Music in Schools

Department of Education and Science

Education Pamphlet Number 27

Her Majesty's Stationery Office 1969

First published 1956

Second Edition 1969

SBN 11 270088 8

ii

Contents

The Department of Education and Science is grateful to the many voluntary bodies that offered advice in the preparation of this pamphlet. We would also like to thank the schools and local education authorities that supplied photographs of various aspects of their work.

iv

Introduction

There have been great changes in the musical scene since the first edition of this pamphlet appeared in 1956. Transistors have made music a portable commodity. The audience for an opera or celebrity concert on television can run to millions. On sound there is a continuous programme of good music for most hours of the day. Sales of tape recorders, record players and gramophone records, classical as well as pop, have risen enormously. Beat groups and the more sophisticated folk groups have created a great demand for musical instruments of the more popular kind. Public expenditure on music through the Arts Council and local authorities has increased considerably. In the sphere of higher education, several new music departments in universities have come into being, new buildings are being planned or have already been built for colleges of music in the City of London, Manchester, Birmingham and Huddersfield, accommodation for music has been radically improved in colleges of education throughout the country, and a number of new music centres have been established to satisfy local needs.

In schools there has been a notable development of creative music-making and instrumental playing, and in ways of testing musical experience and knowledge. On the whole, however, music has changed less in schools than it has done outside, partly because ideas take time to crystallise but mainly because facilities for musical work have not kept pace with fast developing needs. As the Newsom Report *Half Our Future* said in 1963, 'Music is frequently the worst equipped and accommodated subject in the curriculum. It is only very recently that specific accommodation for music has begun to be included in the design of school buildings: half the schools in our survey had none, and another quarter had only makeshift provision contrived within an ordinary classroom, often inconveniently placed in relation to other work going on in surrounding rooms. Of all the 'practical' subjects, it had the least satisfactory provision'.

The future thus holds a double challenge. On the one hand there is a challenge to school authorities to provide, when circumstances permit, the facilities that first-rate musical work demands. On the other there is a challenge to teachers to adapt themselves to rapidly changing circumstances and, through personal musicianship and a realistic sense of priorities, to equip themselves to help in guiding public taste. This pamphlet, which has been substantially revised, offers no easy solution to these problems. It does, however, lay down some broad principles which have guided successful education in music in the past and which, examined and renewed in terms of modern conditions, may still prove helpful to those who are willing to interpret them according to their own and their pupils' needs. In considering them it should be remembered that, although new kinds of primary schools, middle schools and secondary schools are now coming into being, musical education is a continuous process which should develop naturally and without interruption from one stage to the next.

1

Traditions

In the grammar, chantry and song schools of the Middle Ages most of the boys received practical training in ecclesiastical song as part of their equipment for a clerical life. A small boy like Chaucer's 'litel clergeon' of seven, listening to the older boys rehearsing their *Alma redemptoris*, and learning it by rote from one of them who could explain only the general sense of the words ('I lerne song, I can but smal grammere') might—but for untoward accidents—look forward to the university, where he could extend both his theoretical know-ledge and his practical skill, as did Nicolas the 'Clerk of Oxenford' with his

> gay sautrye
> On which he made a nightes melodye
> So swetely, that al the chambre rong;
> And Angelus ad Virginem he song . . .

Such informal music-making would give both point and relief to the theoretical treatise of Boethius *De institutione Musica* that formed the basis of musical study in the *quadrivium* or second part of the arts degree. In a narrower sense, the modern counterpart of these young 'academics' is found among the gifted children who specialise in music while at school and afterwards go on to a college of music or a university. In a wider sense, we all inherit from the mediaeval schools our concept of song, especially religious song, as a spiritual force binding together the school community on regular or special occa-sions. This use of music is accepted in every school where singing, and often instrumental music also, enters into the ceremonial of the daily act of worship, speech day functions and other times of corpor-ate assembly.

The sixteenth century in England witnessed an enlargement of men's ideas of what makes for a full education, and humanistic writers on the subject made serious claims for the inclusion of musical training, partly on social grounds, but more often because they held in respect the Greek ideal of music as an art which properly understood, taught

1

and practised could help to integrate the personality, bringing into just proportion its physical, mental, moral and emotional elements.

Whether the Tudor grammar schools normally provided either theoretical or practical instruction in music is doubtful. Much depended on the headmaster's personal interests, then even more than now. James Whitelocke, a pupil at Merchant Taylors' School in the second half of the sixteenth century, recalled that Mulcaster, besides teaching him Hebrew, Greek and Latin, took pains 'to increase my skill in musique, in whiche I was brought up by dayly exercise in it as in singing and playing upon instruments'.[1] Few can have gone as far as John Howes of Christ's Hospital, who considered 'that children should learne to singe, to play uppon all sorts of instruments, as to sound the trumpett, the cornett, the recorder, or flute, to play uppon shagbolts, shalmes, and all other instruments that are to be plaid uppon either with winde or finger'.[2] The statutes of Westminster School for 1560 provided for two weekly lessons in music, each of an hour's duration, 'as a knowledge of singing is found to be of the greatest use for clear and distinct enunciation'.[3]

But in the main the secularization of schools during the sixteenth century reduced the number of children who received regular musical training as part of the school curriculum. The monasteries were dissolved, most of the chantries confiscated, and a number of collegiate foundations converted into cathedrals with song schools devoted entirely to the training of choristers. The separation of song school from grammar school was to result in a neglect of music in the latter almost down to the present day.[4] The widespread musical culture of Englishmen and Englishwomen in the sixteenth and seventeenth centuries was almost entirely the product of private tuition and domestic practice, though it is probable that many of their teachers learnt the rudiments in the surviving choir schools. And in a few girls' schools there seem to have been serious musical studies: Josiah Priest's boarding school, for which Purcell wrote *Dido and Aeneas* (about 1689), and Mrs. Perwich's in Hackney, with the

---

[1] *Musical Education in Tudor Times*. David G. T. Harris: (Proceedings of the Musical Association, 1938–9, p. 121.) Mulcaster's views on the place of music in a school curriculum are set out in his *Positions* (1581) and *The First Part of the Elementarie* (1582).

[2] Ibid, p. 122.

[3] Ibid, p. 120. See also *Music and poetry of the English Renaissance*, Bruce Pattison 1948.

[4] It is now usual for a cathedral choir school to be organised either as a preparatory or as a secondary school with a majority of boys who are not choristers. Certain of these schools have developed a musical bias. Where no choir school survives or has ever existed, the choristers frequently hold places in neighbouring maintained or direct grant schools.

renowned Susanna Perwich[5] as the leader among several musical pupils, were outstanding seventeenth century examples.

On the whole, however, the ethical concept of music as a humanising influence tended to dwindle towards the close of the seventeenth and throughout the eighteenth century, though it never disappeared completely from educational thought. It was replaced by a guarded tolerance of the art as a pastime or at best a relaxation from weightier studies. Early in the humanistic period Elyot had emphasised both the recreational and ethical values of music, basing his doctrine on that of Plato's *Republic:*

'The tutor suffereth not the childe to be fatigate with continual studie or lernynge . . . but that there may be entrelased and mixte therewith some pleasant lernynge and exercise as playenge on instruments of musike . . . seeing how necessary it is for the better attaining the knowledge of the public weal, which containeth a perfect harmony.'[6]

Milton expanded the same idea in recommending music as a form of relief to an overloaded curriculum, in a passage prophetic of modern lunch-hour activities:

'The interim of . . . rest before meat may . . . be taken up in recreating and composing their travail'd spirits with the solemn and divine harmonies of Musick heard or learnt; either while the skilful Organist plies his grave and fancied descant, in lofty fugues, or the whole Symphony with artful and unimaginable touches adorn and grace the well studied chords of some choice Composer, sometimes the Lute, or soft Organ stop waiting on elegant Voices either to Religious, martial or civil Ditties; which if wise men and prophets be not extreamly out, have a great power over dispositions and manners, to smooth and make them gentle from rustick harshness and distemper'd passions. The like also would not be unexpedient after Meat to assist and cherish Nature in his first concoction and send their minds back to study in good tune and satisfaction.'[7]

[5] *The Virgins Pattern* 1661: John Batchiler.
  'Ask Rogers, Bing, Coleman and others
  The most exactly skilful Brothers:
  Ask Brian, Mell, Ives, Gregories,
  Howes, Stifkins, all, in whom there lyes
  Rare Arts of Musick, they can tell,
  How well she sang: how rarely well
  She play'd on several instruments.'
[6] *The Boke named the Governour*, 1531: Sir Thomas Elyot.
[7] *Tractate of Education*, 1644, reprinted 1673: Milton.

Once separated from its philosophical context, the 'recreational' theory was capable of doing much harm. If music was nothing more than a means of relaxation or a pastime it was unworthy of a place among serious studies. Even the scholarly Dr. Burney could describe the art as 'an innocent luxury, unnecessary, indeed, to our existence, but a great improvement and gratification of the sense of hearing',[8] though elsewhere[9] he defended the 'uselessness' of music on the ground that the same had been said about electricity, which apart from Franklin's lightning conductor and some attested therapeutic value 'has never yet, with much certainty, been applied by its discoverers to any useful purpose.'

The unhappy divorce between music and the humanities that began before Burney's own age and continued, as far as England was concerned, until late in the nineteenth century, helped to banish music from most boys' schools and degrade it to the level of an 'accomplishment' in boarding schools for girls. The sternest and most contemptuous dismissal of practical music from the company of serious studies was uttered by John Henry (later Cardinal) Newman:[10]

> 'Recreations are not education; accomplishments are not education. . . You may as well call drawing and fencing education, as a general knowledge of botany and conchology. Stuffing birds or playing stringed instruments is an elegant pastime, and a resource to the idle, but it is not education; it does not form or cultivate the intellect.'

What restored music to the schools was the recognition of its educative values by the great educational reformers of the eighteenth and nineteenth centuries. Rousseau, Pestalozzi and Froebel gave it an honoured place in their systems. All three of them in their different ways insisted on dealing with children as children, and not as adults in miniature. They recognised the importance of drawing upon the kind of music most natural to a young child, the simple folk-song or 'nursery song' fashioned, preserved and orally transmitted by generations of women occupied in tending and playing with their children. They also grasped the value of spontaneity in singing: it was observed that the pupils of Pestalozzi sang on all possible occasions, and especially when out of doors.

---

[8]Introduction (Definitions) to *A General History of Music* (1776): Charles Burney.

[9]Introduction to *The Present State of Music in France and Italy* (1771): Charles Burney.

[10]*The Idea of a University*, 1852 (Discourse VI): J. H. Newman.

The development of these educational ideas coincided with the period when scholars, poets and musicians in various countries, and especially the German-speaking ones, were collecting and studying folk-songs and learning to appreciate their strong simplicity. Although the hidden wealth of English folk-song was still ignored, the value of song not merely as a recreation but also as a humanising and ennobling influence was accepted by leading thinkers in this country before the period of compulsory education. In Robert Owen's school at the New Lanark Mills the children sang Scottish traditional songs and took part in traditional dances. Within a year or so of the passing of the Forster Act in 1870, singing was made virtually a compulsory subject of elementary education in all Board schools, one-sixth of the annual grant being payable only if singing was included in the school curriculum. To be eligible for this proportion of the grant the school had to prepare a dozen songs in the course of the year and sing to the inspector those he asked for. The Code of 1882 introduced a grant of sixpence a pupil if the singing were 'by rote' and a shilling if a successful attempt were made to teach the elements of notation.

The energy with which the teaching profession applied itself to the task of making the nation's children musically literate can perhaps be realised best from a perusal of inspectors' general reports published during the last three decades of the nineteenth century.[11] At first some districts were more successful than others. An inspector working in Yorkshire could write as early as 1873: 'Singing is taught in all the schools except one, and is generally done well, as indeed it ought to be in the West Riding where the people have a genius for singing'.[12] From another area in the same year the report was more guarded: Attention has lately been devoted to vocal music. Singing has never been wholly neglected, and here and there it deserved the name of music; but generally speaking singing was executed with a curious indifference to pitch, or tune or style ... If vocal beauties were obscured defects were happily hidden by the thunder of the harmonium. I cannot say that this description is altogether out of date, though a great and successful effort has been made to improve ... The possibilities of school singing are beginning to reveal themselves. Singing by ear no longer means the slovenly rendering of debased melodies, all possibly in the same key; but it means an ability to appreciate accurately, and reproduce with flexibility and exactness,

---

[11]For other examples of the provision of opportunities for musical education during the earlier years of the Industrial Revolution, see *A Social History of English Music*, London 1964. Chapter 4. E. D. Mackerness.

[12]Reports of the Committee of Council on Education, 1873–74, p. 55.

and compass of voice enlarged by practice, music which abides in the memory from hearing it or seeing it notated . . .'[13]

Inspectors at this period were required to investigate the merits of the various methods of teaching sight-singing they found in the schools. One produced a classification of prevailing methods under three headings: the 'fixed Do' or Italian system, as used in several continental countries today, which received powerful support from John Hullah; the 'movable Do' or 'Lancashire sol-fa'; and the 'tonic solfa' method associated with the name of John Curwen, the Congregational minister who from the middle of the century onwards had disseminated his ideas through lectures, classes and text books.

Few of Curwen's teaching devices were original: the modulator, the French time-names, and the solfa syllables were all taken over from other (and, in the case of the pitch-names, much older) systems. His work lay in the direction of synthesis; he fused established principles and effective devices into a logical scheme of aural training that could be handled by a competent teacher with a minimum knowledge of music, and understood by pupils who had no instrumental experience. Curwen always insisted that tonic solfa was a system of *aural training*; and those who watched the spread of his ideas in the schools generally agreed that the effect of his method when ably taught was to make the children sing better, and above all sing in tune. It was also emphasised, both in the writings of Curwen himself and in the later *Codes* and *Suggestions* issued by the Board of Education, that the special notation of tonic solfa was intended only as a series of stepping stones to the reading of staff notation.

One inspector who claimed to know little of music summed up the whole situation—perhaps for the future as well as his own time—by expressing 'a hope that no amount of knowledge of the meaning and value of any musical notation may be accepted as fully satisfactory, unless the children can sing their songs in a pleasing manner and with correct method and also interpret an unseen piece of easy music'.[14]

The development of singing in the schools undoubtedly gained impetus not only from official interest but also from the intense choral activity that was going on throughout the country. John Hullah, one of the pioneers of class-singing instruction among adults, was able to write in 1873: 'A singing class, a choir, or a choral society is now to be met with in every town, almost in every village.'

---

[13]Ibid, p. 187.
[14]Reports of the Committee of Council on Education, 1882–3, p. 410. For a more detailed account of the development of music in the national system of elementary education, see Mackerness, *op. cit.*, Chapter 5 *The Victorian Era: National Education and Musical Progress.*

This enthusiasm was reflected in the training colleges for intending teachers where, from the time of his appointment (1872) as inspector of music in those institutions, Hullah gave practical as well as theoretical tests from which few were exempt. His reports on training college music are filled with observations that have more than ephemeral value: 'The business of the teacher (tutor) in a training college is not (save incidentally) to form a pleasing choir, but a body of vocal musicians, every individual member of which shall be able to teach vocal music .... 'As a rule, teachers sing too much, in practical lessons; and they talk too much, and play or sing—or make their pupils do so—too little in a theoretical one. In a word, no so-called theoretical lesson should pass without practice; no practical lesson without theory' .... 'A skilful teacher may, and often does, give a clever and useful lesson on something with which yesterday he was comparatively unacquainted .... But the most elementary singing lesson involves, on the part of him who gives it, *a sympathy of eye and ear* that can be attained only by long cultivation, can be made available only when it has become part of his being; and when thus attained and made available, can no more be lost or forgotten, like the knowledge of mere facts, than the power of speaking or understanding his native tongue'.[15]

The chief obstacle to progress in school singing was the lack of suitable songs, especially for the younger children. Much of the material contained in school song books was adapted from German sources, or specially written; and the original matter was frequently banal, in either tunes or words or both. Soon after the middle of the century, however, the publication of Chappell's *Popular Music of the Olden Time* called attention to a vast amount of English song preserved in printed form, and included works by known composers—especially those of the eighteenth century—which have become part of the national heritage; and a series of school song books, of which Hullah's published in 1866 was one of the best, drew upon Chappell for English material and also on Thomson's *Scottish Songs*, Thomas's *Welsh Melodies* and Bunting's *Ancient Music of Ireland*. Shortly after the turn of the century the Board of Education gave official backing to a song repertory based on these traditional sources. Its *Suggestions for the Consideration of Teachers*, first published in 1905, included as an appendix a lengthy list of recommended English, Scottish, Welsh and Irish songs, with a few rounds. These 'national songs' soon afterwards formed the basis of a school song book, originally edited by C.V. (later Sir Charles) Stanford, that is still widely used. It was unfortunate that the list appeared a little too early to take into

---

[15]Reports of the Committee of Council on Education, 1872–3, pp. 362 seq., 1873–4, pp. 285 seq.

account the influence of the movement for collecting folk-song from
oral as opposed to printed sources. The first volume of *Folk Songs
from Somerset* had been published by Cecil Sharp at the end of 1904;
two years later he wrote to the press criticising the choice of songs set
out in the 1905 *Suggestions*. 'Schoolmasters' he protested, 'in belief
that they are teaching folksongs, will give the children the songs
suggested in the Blue book . . . . '[16] Stanford defended the *Suggestions*
list on the ground that it was better to 'begin with a list of those
(songs) which have long been acknowledged as the backbone of
national music'; Sharp insisted that it was important to distinguish
'between two kinds of music that are fundamentally different from
one another . . . . the one is individual, the other communal and
racial'.

Within a few years the publication of several collections of folk-songs
taken from oral transmission, of further collections of 'national'
songs, and of several books that drew impartially on both kinds of
source, gave teachers a wealth of fine material for unison singing
from the infant school onward, and the repertory of traditional song,
augmented not only from British but also from American and European sources, is still increasing. Further, the interest taken by leading
musicians in the work of the schools has enriched the literature of
unison and part singing in a measure that few other countries can
rival. The rise of the school music festival[17] brought first-class composers and conductors into closer touch with the elementary schools,
and led not only to a rapid improvement in standards of singing but
also to the composition of music for children's voices, much of it,
particularly in the *genre* of part-songs for equal voices, of a fine order
of artistry.

The expansion of secondary education in the early years of the
twentieth century led to fresh developments. The Board's Memorandum on *Music in the Secondary School*, issued in 1906, was a slender
document, stressing what might be rather than what normally
existed at this time in the secondary school. Confidence in the
achievements of the elementary school appears in the recommendations of the teaching of notation: 'It is not generally appreciated,
except in the Elementary School, that sight singing can easily be begun
at about the same age as reading and writing, and that the difficulty,
as with these subjects, increases out of all proportion if the beginning
is unduly postponed.' And the Memorandum draws attention to the

---

[16]*Cecil Sharp*, A. H. Fox-Strangeways: 1933. See also *A Guide to English Folk
Song Collections*, Margaret Dean-Smith, 1954, pages 14–16, for an excellent
summary of this controversy.

[17]The Association of Competitive Festivals was founded in 1905: the British
Federation of Music Festivals in 1921. The Non-competitive Festival Movement
began in 1927.

1905 *Suggestions* list of songs, with the observation: 'It is generally recognised that the traditional song literature of a nation is the natural foundation on which musical culture should be based. Such songs are the true classics of the people, and their survival, some of them by oral tradition alone, shows that their appeal is direct and lasting'.

Yet it was from the secondary school, and from its oldest and reputedly most conservative representatives, that some of the most valuable ideas for the growth of school music were to come. Beginning with Uppingham, where Thring in 1861 made history by appointing a Director of Music,[18] several of the independent public schools had been developing their musical lives in a manner that differed considerably from what was possible at this period in schools supported or aided by the State. With larger financial resources, a more flexible school day, and teams of highly qualified specialist teachers, some of them men of outstanding personal qualities, they were able to build up musical traditions that included individual instrumental tuition, school orchestras, chamber music groups, house music competitions, and chapel services combining in a distinctive way collegiate with congregational singing. Most important of all, perhaps, they demonstrated that the classics of musical literature, if skilfully graded and presented, could make a strong and lasting appeal to the average boy. As the following chapters will show, there are few of these features that have not been embodied in some form in the musical life of the country's schools as a whole, while the independent schools in their turn have often been ready to learn from the experience of the younger state schools, especially in the field of class-teaching.

During the first half century that has elapsed since the issue of the first *Suggestions* and the first Secondary School Memorandum, school music has enlarged its scope so widely that a brief survey can indicate only a few important trends. These may be summarised under the headings of instrumental music, movement in association with music, and training in listening. It is interesting to note that all three, though generally regarded as products of a modern educational outlook, were foreshadowed by nineteenth century pioneers of universal education and indeed can be traced back to still older experiments, as historical references already given in this chapter may have shown.

When we read of the amount of instrumental music cultivated in the training colleges of the seventies—ranging from piano classes to students' performances, at the annual inspection, on a variety of

---

[18]This term was not in fact used in connection with the original appointment of a 'music master'.

instruments including the cornet and the bagpipe chanter,[19] or of school bands having been established (by 1882) in many boys' schools, where they were said to 'give much pleasure and amusement not only to the performers but to all the children in the school',[20] we realise that the present day cultivation of instrumental playing in schools of every type is a modern fulfilment of earlier ideals. John Howes of Christ's Hospital[21] would find no more than the realisation of his dreams if he could return from the sixteenth century to overhear a school orchestra rehearsing today; he might indeed gain satisfaction from observing that percussion playing can be a valuable element in the teaching of backward children, since the records of Christ's Hospital contain the following entry: 'Drommes. Paid to George Kinge, and George Pulliard, drommers to her Mtie for iij dromes to instruct the ignorant sort of children . . . not apt for theire book, and for theire better preferment in her Mtie affaires when tyme shall serve, the sum of £03 12s. 0d.'[22] If the 'musical drill' of the early elementary schools has long been superseded by infinitely more flexible systems of relationship between music and bodily movement, some of which are still at stages of vigorous experiment, it was fundamentally a reaching back towards educational principles established in the ancient Greek world.

When Matthew Arnold, writing as an inspector of schools in the eighteen-seventies, expressed the hope that 'music, now that instruction in it is made universal, ought to lay the foundation in the children of our elementary schools of a cultivated power of perception.'[23] he might have been anticipating the tremendous widening of musical experience brought about half a century later by the coming of the gramophone, the radio and the sound film. On the other hand, an early eighteenth century amateur had already given a warning, in a homely simile, against the misconceived kind of 'musical appreciation' that substitutes verbal descriptive or analytical treatment for direct contact through performance: 'And grant that a man read all the books of musick that ever were wrote, I shall not allow that musick is or can be understood out of them, no more than the taste of meats out of cookish receipt books'.[24]

This principle, however phrased in contemporary terms, remains true today. Actual experience of learning and making music is

---

[19]Report on inspection of music in training colleges, 1873.
[20]Report of H.M.I. for S. Dorset and S.W. Hampshire, 1882.
[21]Ibid, page 2.
[22]Quoted in *The School Drama in England*. T. H. Vail Motter: London, 1929, p. 173.
[23]Report of the Committee of Council on Education, 1872–3, p. 24.
[24]*The Musicall Gramarian*, Roger North: (1728). Ed. Hilda Andrews, London, 1925.

essential at every stage, from nursery school to university, from the first attempts at instrumental playing to the training of professional musicians. 'Cookish receipt books' (and the personal guidance of practised and discerning cooks) are indispensable in their place and season, but they are no more than means to an end—the practice and enjoyment of living music.

2

Primary Schools

Basic Experience

When a child first comes to school he normally brings with him a considerable variety of musical experience. Much of this will doubtless have come from sound radio and television programmes ranging in suitability from such series as *Listen with Mother* to material of a more sophisticated character preferred by the older members of the family. Snatches of contemporary popular song heard at home and in the street will also have made their impression. Some children may have come from homes where music is a respected part of everyday life, where the adults or older children play instruments, or where the mother is able to pass on the nursery songs that form the one section of our native folk-song that has never entirely disappeared from oral tradition. There will be few who have not become aware of the raw materials of music, the differences in quality of sound and volume that result from tapping, banging and twanging various objects, and of the satisfaction of improvising rhythms by such primitive means.

It is the particular task of the nursery or infant school to develop the most valuable elements in these early experiences and to enlarge the scope of musical activity, including experiments with sound, in ways that will create a desire to acquire musical skills and thereby explore the world of music to the limits of individual capacity. To achieve these aims, initially, there need be no formal instruction in lesson periods specifically devoted to music; indeed this could be out of harmony with modern nursery and infant school practice. The more freely music can enter into the daily life of small children the better, and their own teacher, working in the normal surroundings of her room, is in the best position to realise at what points in the school day some kind of musical activity is possible and appropriate, whether the whole group or a few individual members of it should take part, and what materials are required.

A suitably equipped music corner is valuable for this work. It could be in the classroom, in a corridor or in a hall—anywhere that

12

provides free access for individual children or small groups—and it might contain simple instruments such as tambourines, drums, melodic percussion instruments including xylophones, glockenspiels and chime bars, and also appropriate visual material, including tunes in staff notation. The variety of instruments will enable the children to discover experimentally a great deal about pitch relationship, tone quality and differences of volume; percussion instruments, especially, can be used in connection with movement, dramatic work and singing, although the melodic experience obtainable through instruments like the xylophone, which produce sounds of definite and graduated pitch, should be regarded as at least equal in importance with purely rhythmic percussion. This sort of basic experience and the natural developments from it are desirable for all, but particularly for the child of exceptional ability who may later become a performer, as they may help to condition him against the danger of playing mechanically from the notes.

Creative Music Making

Through experiments of this kind children develop a desire to improvise and create music of their own. The film *Our Own Music*, which is available on sale from the British Broadcasting Corporation or on loan from the Educational Foundation for Visual Aids, indicates the scope of original creative work that can develop throughout the primary school. Initially, this work may be based upon a restricted choice of notes, as in the earlier stages of the method evolved by Carl Orff, but, in course of time, some children will become more adventurous and try to use additional notes in their improvisations. Naturally they should be encouraged to do so and should not be held back in order to conform with any pre-arranged system of instruction. As in all creative work, hints or suggestions may often be needed; indeed one of the chief functions of the resourceful teacher is to open the pupils' eyes to the possibilities that lie before them.

In exploring these possibilities use may be made of suitable published material or of sound and television broadcasts for schools such as *Music Workshop* or *Making Music*. For the most part, however, ideas should suggest themselves. A simple percussion accompaniment might be made for a song that is already known, or the teacher might stimulate a sound-effect by giving a visual or a word picture of some kind. More sophisticated arrangements and original compositions will emerge as the children grow up and learn about music in other ways and, ultimately, some of them may come to record their work in musical notation. At all stages beyond the earliest experiments with sound, it is a great incentive to give the young practising musician some useful function to perform—for instance, a tune might be required for a hymn that one of them has written, or an instrumental interlude might be needed for a play. The functional use of music has an important place in every school today.

Movement is a form of creative activity that can be so closely related to music as to become inseparable from it. The general question of movement to music is considered on pages 19–20. It is sufficient here to emphasise the creative influence that music exerts on movement and, perhaps even more to the point, the stimulus that movement can give to music. At its simplest, a rhythm on a single percussion instrument can suggest a dance, but a dance can also suggest a rhythm, in which case the percussion player needs just as much perception and resource as if he were creating a rhythm of his own. In using movement as a creative medium it is important to remember this two-way communication and to provide adequate opportunities for creative dance to stimulate musical imagination. Obviously, there are almost unlimited possibilities in connection with mime and drama.

Re-creative Music Making

Although the importance of providing opportunities for original experimental and creative work can hardly be over-emphasised, most musical activity at both the professional and amateur levels is concerned not with creating new music but with re-creating (i.e. performing) music which already exists. In this respect music differs from the visual and the plastic arts and this was the aspect of the work that received most attention in the past. Although that attention may sometimes have been excessive, it is still desirable that as children get older re-creative music-making should normally occupy an increasing proportion of their time. The artistic satisfaction obtainable from reproducing something beautiful can be of lasting benefit to the sensitive child, and this satisfaction is often enhanced if he takes part in re-creating music with others. At first this may be no more than singing a nursery song unaccompanied or playing a singing game. Later, at the top of the junior or middle school, children may take part in performing a substantial work, a cantata perhaps, involving part-singing and instrumental accompaniment.

At every stage it is important that they should be called upon to re-create only the best. Indeed it is probably more necessary in this generation than in any other that schools should set high standards of taste. Amongst the surfeit of material available, however, choosing the right music is sometimes a difficulty. If in doubt, it is advisable to appraise it in the first place from the adult's, rather than the child's, point of view. To pass muster for children, music should first be acceptable to a reasonably sophisticated adult audience on its artistic merits alone. Only after it has passed this test should its suitability be considered on other grounds. A traditional nursery song would almost certainly pass such a test on grounds both of quality and suitability, whereas some songs specially composed for children, although superficially appropriate, might fail on grounds of quality. Groups of teachers meeting together, say, to arrange a festival might sometimes apply this test in a practical way, and they should remember that, even if 'the children like it', inferior music (and also inferior words) should be resolutely excluded from their list. There is plenty of good music that they would enjoy even more, and it is part of a music teacher's responsibility, arising from his or her freedom of choice, to select it.

Another reason for avoiding the 'childish' approach is that children are often capable of tackling far more advanced music than is sometimes supposed. The fact that a simple traditional nursery song may be suitable for the infant school should by no means exclude songs by Schubert and Mozart, and in the instrumental field home-made arrangements from Stravinsky and Bartók should not be regarded as beyond quite young children's scope. This process of extending their vision should be continued throughout the junior and middle school until, at the top, they have acquired a considerable repertoire of fine songs and have been introduced, through simple forms of actual participation, to some first-rate chamber and orchestral music.

Having discovered great music in this way and obtained the satisfaction of re-creating it themselves, children can extend their understanding by listening to performances by adults, either on the radio or gramophone or, better still, by the teacher or at a concert of some kind.

Listening to Music

Children's capacity to listen can be developed by practice, both as performers and as audience. As performers, they should be trained to listen carefully to themselves, in relation to the performance of the other children in the group. At its simplest this kind of listening will help to cure the occasional 'growler' amongst the younger ones, whilst at a more advanced level it will assist good intonation in a recorder ensemble. It is a help in this connection to keep the singing or playing fairly soft and to avoid disturbing concentration by an obtrusive accompaniment. Listening as a performer should also embrace a feeling for phrasing and a sensitive response to nuances of dynamics and rhythm. Mechanical percussion playing in which emphasis is placed upon reading from charts rather than careful listening has no value artistically and may, indeed, actually blunt a child's sensitivity.

Children's experience of music as outside listeners begins before they come to school and should continue indefinitely throughout their school careers. Even when music is played with the intention of evoking a response in movement, it may be found that some prefer to sit quietly and listen. This preference should be respected, and for all of them there should be frequent opportunities to listen to short pieces played by the teacher on the piano, the recorder, or the violin, from gramophone records, or from broadcasts. Many of the shorter and simpler classics are admirably suited to this purpose, as are certain modern works such as the children's pieces of Béla Bartók. It is quite unnecessary that music presented to children should have associations with a story or a picture, or that they should be encouraged to visualise such associations. The range of music they find interesting is commonly underestimated; on the other hand, their span of attention is short and should not be stretched unduly. Once they have heard something they enjoy they will welcome it again and again, and the familiarity that comes from frequent re-hearing is an important factor in forming sound and pleasurable habits of listening.

Opportunities for listening should continue in the junior and middle school along with active music-making. The widest possible variety of live performance is to be desired, as long as it is competent; and recordings and broadcasts are invaluable provided that the quality of reproduction is good. The various series of school music broadcasts on sound and television offer a refreshing enlargement of repertory and a range of resources not easily available in the classroom. It is important that close attention should be paid to the age-range for which they are planned, and that the pupils should have copies of the appropriate pamphlets, which are cheap and attractive, and still have value after the series of broadcasts is ended. In some village schools, where each teacher copes with a wide age-range, groups of children may listen without her aid. Every primary teacher will also find it worthwhile to discuss with them the music they hear out of school, especially through sound broadcasting and television programmes, as only by doing so can he appreciate his pupils' cultural background. Particular care is needed, however, to avoid any suggestion that the music they hear at home is poor or that the teacher is trying to win them over to something better. His interest is all that is required.

Singing

The preceding paragraphs have been concerned with the main aspects of music in primary schools in their broadest senses. Certain lines along which the practical work might be developed are now considered in greater detail.

Singing rightly comes foremost among the resources available at any time in the day; it depends on no apparatus apart from the human voice, and experience shows that there are few teachers of young children who cannot learn to sing simply, naturally, and rhythmically the traditional songs that are their heritage and which should form the basis of all musical training at the primary stage.

Even if the teacher is a pianist she should cultivate the practice of unaccompanied singing, which allows her to get closer to the children both physically and imaginatively, though she may find an instrument, which need not invariably be the piano, an aid to ensuring that the pitch of the song is suited to the range of the children's voices. An increasing number of teachers are now using the guitar, which can provide a light, sympathetic accompaniment whilst allowing a close vocal contact with the children.

It is best to present a simple song as a whole, without separating words from tune, and the teacher will be able to do this with more confidence if she has memorised it. As the songs become longer it may be necessary to teach them phrase by phrase, a method that helps towards an appreciation of the rhythmic shape of the song and towards breath control, but piecemeal presentation must always be avoided. Formal exercises in breathing and tone formation are seldom effective with small children; musical phrasing and pleasing tone develop through imitation of good patterns set by the teacher and by the more talented members of the group.

For infants, many excellent books of traditional English nursery songs, with others adapted from foreign sources, are now available and schools should have a wide selection. Thirty or forty different song books are by no means too many to possess, indeed some schools have many more. Some of the most useful books suffer from overloaded piano accompaniments, which can either be omitted or simplified, or possibly rearranged for the guitar or for a few percussion instruments. Many simple folk songs lend themselves to antiphonal singing between teacher and children or between one group of children and another, and some give scope for taking the parts of different characters. Songs by modern composers may be added to this wealth of traditional song-literature as the children grow older, but great care is needed in selecting them; there is much poorly written or dull material to be avoided, and some of the best can only be effective if a really capable pianist is available. Unlike the specially written 'action songs' in which every step and gesture is prescribed and any initiative precluded, traditional singing games have a perennial vitality.

Children at the junior stage, as at the nursery and infant stages, learn mainly by imitating the singing of their teacher. Without discarding the nursery rhymes and songs they have already learnt, they should explore the treasures of the national and folk music of their own and other lands. Towards the top of the junior school they may widen their repertory by judicious choice from classical and modern composers and learn, first through antiphonal singing and later through canons, rounds and descants, something of the joy of part-singing. Much of their singing at all stages should be unaccompanied, so that they sense the need for easy and beautiful tone, true vowels, lively lips, vital rhythm and flexibility in shaping the contour of phrases. The mood of the song must be realised first of all, for interpretation is the target at which all technical skills, and even accuracy of notes, are aimed. It is a mistake to try to 'learn the song' first and subsequently 'put in the expression', or to separate words and tune during the first stages of the learning process. Children love contrast of mood and speed—light, fast 'lip-songs' are a particular delight—but pitch and tempo should be congenial to the range of their voices and their natural rate of movement.

Many hymn books, not specially edited for use in schools, print the tunes in keys chosen to allow baritones in the congregation to sing the melody in comfort; some hymns may therefore need to be transposed as much as a third higher for children. Even a good song book may contain tunes that are all the better for an upward trans-position to a key that is more suitable for young voices. It is equally necessary to select a suitable tempo and to keep it so clearly in mind that it can be set with certainty and conviction in a few introductory bars (which may come from the final phrase of the song). Uncertainty of tempo, in fact, is one of the commonest causes of indifferent singing at all stages, from the infant to the secondary school.

The inability of some children, frequently boys, to sing in tune is a defect that is often described as 'droning' or 'growling'. It is com-monly caused either by difficulties of muscular co-ordination or by faulty listening; it is seldom a sign of true tone-deafness, which occurs in only a minute fraction of the population, nor is it to be regarded as a symptom of being unmusical. On the contrary, the 'droner', not always conscious of his defective pitch-adjustment, is often enthusiastic to an embarrassing degree. Despite this embarrass-ment, he should never be excluded from the singing class, as some-times happened in the past, or silenced altogether when the others are singing. Given the freedom to sing as a normal member of the group, perhaps in proximity to good singers, and encouraged to listen attentively, he will probably gain better control of his voice by the time he is eight or nine years old.

The 'droner' generally has a normally developed rhythmic sense and can take part in percussion playing, and at the top infant stage his sense of pitch may be helped considerably by playing any simple melodic instrument. The presence of several 'droners' in one group is an almost certain sign that the group has heard and taken part in singing too infrequently, and the remedy is obvious. In dealing with the whole problem it is comforting to reflect that the pitch intervals of our musical system are to some extent arbitrary, and that no child is born knowing them; they are learnt by imitation, like the sounds and intonations of the mother tongue, and the process takes longer for some than for others. A little remedial group work in singing can be as helpful as it often is in reading.

Movement

The combination of movement with music has been the subject of much experiment, expecially in primary schools, and the whole question calls for clear thinking and continued study. It can take the crude form of fitting paces to the regular beats of a march. It can denote a fixed pattern of simple steps to a dance tune, a relationship that is pre-determined when the music and the movement have evolved together, as in folk dances. Or the relationship may be less precise, as when movement follows the general structure of a piece of music—its phrase-lengths, its climaxes and cadences and so on—without attempting to reproduce its metrical pattern. It may even be based almost entirely on an emotional parallelism, with movement of a free character generated in response to a conception of the prevailing mood of the music. In recent years encouraging progress has been made towards this understanding of the relationship of music to the movement lesson. For instance, awareness of a specific quality, such as 'strong' and 'angular', can often be sharpened by listening to and then moving to music which has these characteristics. Electronic sound recordings have proved helpful in work of this kind.

It is often assumed that all children move spontaneously to music that attracts them, but experience shows that they vary in this respect, some having real difficulty in making any kind of response in movement except in a limited way and with conventional steps. For this reason, music may be a hindrance rather than a stimulus to movement. On the other hand, music that dictates an easily-grasped metrical pattern, like that of traditional tunes, may give scope for individuality if the children are encouraged to carry out the pattern according to their own ideas, whether these lead them to move over a wide area or to confine themselves to a restricted space.

A few clear principles emerge from these somewhat complex considerations. First, too much should not be expected from young children by way of response in movement to music until they have acquired resources for movement apart from musical associations. Secondly, it is not always as easy as it may appear to extract a rhythmic pattern from a musical texture. It may therefore be helpful in the earlier stages to use percussion instruments, rather than gramophone records or piano, to suggest movement, with opportunities for the children to supply their own accompaniment when moving, or to play rhythms for other children to move to. The percussion instruments used must be of British Standards quality, for only an instrument capable of producing a good sound is likely to evoke a satisfactory movement response. Thirdly, any music used for movement, however simple, must be artistically satisfying. Music played with distorted accentuation, or specially written to accompany one narrowly specified type of movement, or amateurish improvisations, should not be tolerated in any scheme of musical training.

The Need for Skills

Instinctive forms of musical expression such as singing and movement, calling for no special equipment and depending upon the natural use of the body or the voice, can bring children immense satisfaction and, for some of them, may be all they need. Others, however, may have the ability and the desire to explore music further for themselves. To obtain access to great music individually they need skills, and these can be acquired only by personal effort and systematic teaching over a considerable time. In teaching these skills, in music as in every other aspect of primary school work, it is necessary to remember that they are simply a means to an end, not an end in themselves, and that they should be constantly applied to situations in which they provide the key to musical experience and enjoyment. Just as the class teacher must balance the claims of grammar and of fluency in written English, of arithmetical accuracy and mathematical understanding, of the chronological sequence of events and vivid historical insight, so in music he must decide how much attention he should give to teaching musical skills (such as music reading or instrumental playing) and how much he should reserve for the joys of creating or re-creating music by more instinctive means. This is a matter that every teacher must settle for himself.

Reading Music

At some time during the infant stage, it may be well worth while to introduce the pitch names (often called 'solfa names') and rhythm names (sometimes termed 'French time names') that have proved their value both in primary and in secondary schools. Unless the teacher thoroughly understands these devices, however, the children will derive little benefit from them. It is important to realise, in the first place, that they are fundamentally aids to the ear; later they can and should be linked with the conventional symbols of ordinary musical notation, but they do not constitute a notation in themselves and should not be treated as such. The whole purpose of the names is to clarify relationships between sounds, and this purpose is defeated if the names are presented as isolated units. They are best introduced in association with easy phrases from tunes the children know, the teacher patterning a phrase of a few notes in which she has substituted pitch or time names for the customary words, and encouraging the children to imitate what she sings as artistically as possible. This involves careful preparation on the teacher's part, and it should be done frequently, a few minutes at a time, as an enjoyable game. The children will soon gain fluency and confidence in sounding the syllables orally, and with consistent practice will find at the junior stage that they already hold the clues to the notation of music.

The introduction of notation in the infant school depends on a number of considerations: how much oral practice it has been possible to give, the children's general ability as indicated by their 'reading ages', and the interest and proficiency of the teacher. Even if no specific teaching of notation is undertaken curiosity may be aroused by placing a few attractive books of tunes in the library or music corner. Creative experience with simple instruments can also provide an incentive to use notation, the situation being real and purposeful.

Once these devices have been translated into the symbols of staff notation—and remarkably few symbols are required to read a very large number of simple tunes—there should be regular and frequent, but not laborious, reading practice. The work of Kodály in Hungary has shown what can be achieved along these lines. The main effort should be towards securing practical fluency, and the temptation to engage in premature explanations of a theoretical nature should be firmly resisted. Much can be taken for granted, at least in the earlier stages and perhaps even in the later ones, by all but the ablest children. There is, for example, no need to avoid keys like E major which are convenient for singing on the assumption that the key-signature must first be elucidated, since all the children need to know is the position of the keynote on the stave. The fact that C major is the easiest key to read on a keyboard instrument, on the other hand, does not imply that it is a particularly easy or grateful key for vocal sight-reading. If attention is given to phrasing and note-values, much of the apparatus of time-signatures and bar lines can be taken in one's stride in reading a simple tune.

As reading power grows it should constantly be brought into service; for instance, the poor intonation that is frequently caused by too flat a leading note in Brahms's *Lullaby* can easily be rectified by a few moments practice on the blackboard in solfa or staff notation—

Example 1.

The first 'readers' in either pitch or rhythm may be anthologies of favourite phrases, the notation of which is recorded by the child with the help of the teacher and with little or no explanation; but as no one can learn to read a language without seeing it often in print, it is essential to provide, at least in the upper half of the junior school and the lower half of the middle school, copies of songs and hymn books with the melody line in staff notation. Some teachers like to use one of the many published sight-reading manuals for supplementary material, whose artistic value is greater if it consists of carefully chosen and graded extracts from song melodies and other musical literature. Reading is an individual matter needing individual exercise and assessment. It is like the teaching of the mother tongue, in which the class teacher finds frequent opportunity to hear a few children read while the rest are otherwise occupied. Reading in chorus gives useful practice but is deceptive without a close knowledge of the stage and rate of progress of each child. Finally, however anxious we may be to develop reading skill at this stage, we should not exclude from the children's repertory songs that are technically too difficult to be incorporated, except perhaps in part, in their reading material. It would be unfortunate if a desirable connection between reading and repertory precluded musical experience with a direct appeal to the ear and the imagination.

A child who plays an instrument such as melodic percussion or the recorder will probably advance more quickly in pitch-reading than with his voice alone. At the same time, a child learning to play any instrument should be taught to hear the expected note mentally before he plays it, rather than strike a bar or tube, press a key, or place his fingers on a string or the holes of a pipe, and thereby produce a sound that may or may not be the one desired.

Instrumental Playing

As mentioned at the beginning of this chapter, children should experiment with playing simple instruments from their earliest days at school. This basic experience is necessary for various reasons. They realise from the start that musical instruments are there to be played, that music comes out of their heads, not out of books, and that making music is more a matter of hearing than seeing. They also learn to listen carefully and fit in with each other. They are thus well on the way to gaining confidence in making music and to playing sensitively before being faced with difficulties of notation. (Schumann's father-in-law, who had a European reputation as a piano teacher, would not allow his pupils to read a note of music until they could play simple pieces artistically by ear; Emanuel Bach, a century before, was equally insistent that artistry should lead technique.) There is no age-limit to this sort of basic instrumental activity and, as occasion offers, it may continue throughout the primary school and, indeed, at secondary and youth club level. In the meantime, from the age of six or seven, a more difficult instrument can be introduced, such as the recorder. This may be used with two distinct aims in mind, either to develop general musical knowledge and ability to read music or to develop instrumental skill with a view to finished performance. Although these two aims are not incompatible it does not necessarily follow that the first will embrace the second; indeed, it is not unusual to find primary schools in which a large number of children have gained valuable knowledge through the use of the recorder as a teaching aid, yet in which no child can play the recorder particularly well as a musical instrument. It is obviously important for the teacher to keep this distinction clearly in mind so that he can assess where, if anywhere, his instrumental work falls short.

Not all children will wish to play a musical instrument in this specialised sense but, if they do, they should have the opportunity of doing so. The recorder can be started in the infant school and, even at this early stage, children should be encouraged to play it artistically with good phrasing and intonation. Quite small groups are essential for successful teaching and the piano should be used sparingly. The guitar, on the other hand, can provide a light accompaniment which need not distract the children from listening carefully, whilst simple unaccompanied part-playing, which should be introduced from the very beginning, will help to establish accurate intonation. As they progress up the junior school and gain both in skill and in finger span, children can tackle more advanced part-playing until they finally join in the full consort, perhaps a guitar or pizzicato cello acting as the bass. By its very nature this is a chamber music rather than an orchestral activity and it needs to be organised as such, but it should be regarded as an essential part of the work if the abler instrumentalists are to progress to the limits of their ability. It does not, at any stage, preclude the use of the descant recorder as a teaching aid or as an orchestral instrument for playing, say, the morning hymn or for accompanying folk dancing.

Strings, particularly the violin, take longer to learn than any other instrument and should therefore be started young. The children's own wishes combined with the teacher's knowledge of their ability in handling easier instruments should enable a reasonable selection of starters to be made. Experience has shown that quite young children, if taught in small groups and encouraged through simple duets to listen for pure intonation, are perfectly capable of playing the violin in tune. The example of the teacher is essential in this respect, as well as in demonstrating tone and style. By no means every school will have a competent violinist on its staff and it will thus be necessary to draw on expertise from outside, a matter that is discussed later in the chapter on Administration. It may be said here, however, that the general music teacher is invaluable in providing stimulus from day to day, in tuning instruments between lessons and organising practising, and in linking up the instrumental work with other aspects of the music of the school. It will obviously help if he has a working know-ledge of the instrument himself, and some teachers have actually learnt the violin alongside their pupils in order to be able to give them guidance of this kind.

One problem that will certainly have to be faced is the widely differ-ent pace at which children progress. If well taught, some will un-doubtedly soon outstrip the others. Groups will thus need to be rearranged or some children may have to be sent elsewhere for lessons, perhaps to a centrally organised music centre or Saturday morning music school. Occasionally a child of quite exceptional ability may be revealed. In that case the phenomenon should be recognised early and special provision, if necessary beyond the Authority's normal resources, should be made, if possible in con-sultation with instrumental teachers of national standing.

Towards the top of the junior school the cello and the viola can be introduced. Some schools, indeed, can boast a string quartet. Some also teach the flute, the clarinet and simple brass such as the cornet, and in certain schools regular instruction is given in the harp. In these schools it is not unusual to find a reasonably well balanced orchestra (perhaps with a member of the staff playing the double bass) in which non-orchestral instruments like recorders, chime-bars and guitars are combined with the more conventional ones and in which the piano, if used at all, is played orchestrally rather than pianistically. Children playing in such an orchestra learn valuable educational disciplines and, through suitable arrangements, can explore a wide repertory of great music. The need to provide these opportunities in primary schools which transfer to secondary schools at the age of 11 is clear. It is also evident, although to a more limited extent, in primary schools which transfer to middle schools at the age of 8 or 9.

The Work as a Whole

It is not easy, in the physical conditions of most primary schools, to reconcile the natural and growing demand of children for disciplined team work with the enormous range of individual interest and ability that becomes increasingly apparent. Instrumental lessons and out-of-class activities, which are nowadays fostered in so many schools, are a great help in giving scope to the keener and more talented and the need for suitable accommodation is reflected in the plans for some new middle schools (see Chapter 8). Combined singing classes and other forms of mass organisation that present the teacher with unwieldy numbers and submerge the individual hopelessly in the group can generally be avoided by judicious planning.

Specialist teaching of certain subjects, including music, has been adopted with intention in some primary schools, and through force of necessity in others. Obviously, if there is a musician of parts on the staff he may help in planning, and in general act as consultant to colleagues and children. He may form a school choir and orchestra, and organise and keep close contact with instrumental work requiring visiting teachers. His room may be a recognised music room suitably sited and equipped for the purpose, even though some other kinds of work may have to go on there. But in any school where there is the desire to let music play its part in an integrated scheme of primary education, free from excessive time-table domination, some parts at least of the teaching must fall to the class teacher, who knows his children individually and can foresee occasions to bring music into touch with other branches of the curriculum. It is hardly necessary to mention that where several teachers are concerned in the teaching of music all should be in possession of the scheme of work for the whole school and that, by consultation and other means, continuity and progression should be ensured, particularly in repertory.

There will be many occasions when music can be brought into relationship with movement, drama, history, art, language, literature, or projects involving interest in work on land or sea; and some of the most fruitful combined work of this character may be carried out in connection with the seasonal festivals. A concert for its own sake has a place, so long as educational interests are not unduly subordinated to impressing audiences. School music festivals have particular value in helping teachers to know what can be achieved in taste, variety and skill. They are exciting events, and so may be incentives to children's keenness, though sometimes they have been allowed to influence unduly, or even to dictate, the musical activities of the schools. (Much the same reservations apply to competitive festivals or eisteddfodau.) Operettas written for children are all too often open to the objection that the quality of the music is poorer than that of the songs they normally sing. One of the most gratifying signs of the times, however, is the notable increase during recent years in the production of dramatic and concert works for young people by contemporary composers of high standing, often in response to festival commissions. There is also a great deal to be said for devising short folk-operas within the school, in which the children can play not only a recreative but an actively creative part. It is unnecessary to emphasise the freshness and variety that music can give to the daily Act of Worship, which may often begin with a short piece of music for quiet listening and include vocal and instrumental contributions by the children themselves.

3

Middle Schools

Experience of middle schools is as yet too limited to enable practical examples to be given of what they might be expected to achieve, but the musical achievements of some independent boys' preparatory schools may point to the possibilities that lie ahead. Vocally these middle years span the average boy's greatest ability to sing, whilst instrumentally they enable uninterrupted progress to be made during a period in which he is best able to lay the foundations of a sound technique. Much the same advantage of continuity may be expected in the new maintained middle schools that are now coming into being, especially if skills such as music reading and instrument playing are begun, if they have not been started already, at the bottom of the school. As with other subjects, music in the middle school should be a natural development from work that has been done before and almost everything that has been said about junior schools in the preceding chapter is equally applicable here. At the top of the middle school more advanced work will naturally be possible and greater demands will be made not only upon the children but upon the teacher and the teaching facilities. The need for specialist knowledge from at least one full-time member of the staff will become more pressing, whilst the help of visiting instrumental teachers may be more urgently required. Similarly more equipment than has customarily been supplied to junior schools may be called for, especially orchestral instruments, whilst additional space for practical work may be needed. Some guidance on these matters is given in Chapter 8.

Although much of the musical work in middle schools may overlap that of the traditional secondary school, it should be regarded more as an extension of primary than a preparation for secondary work. It would be a great pity if the prospect of external examinations were to inhibit the natural growth of middle school music in any way.

4

Secondary Schools

Scope of the Work

The new types of secondary school that are now being established form a variegated pattern which it is impossible to consider as a whole. Each, in its different way, presents new problems as well as offering new opportunities. In considering them it is advisable to keep in mind the main achievements of the past if the most is to be made of developments in the future. A brief description is given in the rest of this section, therefore, of what experience has shown to be the purpose and scope of music at the traditional secondary level, irrespective of organisation. More specific considerations are dealt with later.

Many head teachers of secondary schools have spoken of the beneficial influence which a strong musical tradition has exercised upon the corporate spirit of their school, and there can be few heads nowadays who, if they cannot actually boast as much, do not at least wish that they could say the same. Music enables pupils of all ages and abilities to join together in a corporate effort. It fits many occasions from the daily Act of Worship to the camp fire. It straddles the 'two cultures', demanding great precision yet touching the human spirit. It is both a valuable educational medium and an absorbing hobby. It can illuminate and stimulate effort in other subjects, as it often does in cathedral choir schools. It provides realistic opportunities for work with adults on a footing of equality.

Almost all secondary schools that admit at 11+ provide a basic music course covering the age range 11-14. A good course of this kind should be designed for the pupils as a whole, not merely for those who might subsequently wish to specialise, the purpose being to give the ordinary pupil opportunities to make music up to the limit of his capabilities both creatively and re-creatively, to extend his general musical knowledge and to accustom him to the use of musical notation, at least for reference. Alongside such a course, and stimulated by it, there are often additional opportunities for individual pupils to follow up an interest in music, perhaps by learning an instrument or taking part in voluntary activities such as the production of an opera.

Some schools, especially girls' schools, have retained one or two periods of music in the time-table for all pupils aged 14–16, as in the case of certain other aesthetic subjects, but opinion has been veering in favour of various options at this stage which can be pursued in depth and of which music may be one. Although the selection of one activity for concentrated study naturally implies the rejection of another, there is much to be said for this point of view, provided the basis of selection is as wide as possible, preferably across the whole ability range. Specialised work of this kind often continues at the 16–18 level and can be extended to include an 'A' level course for the few who wish to make a more academic study of music, together with a course in practical musicianship for those who have decided to take up teaching as a career. As young people often wake up to the arts at that age it has also been found advisable to provide a general course aimed at the inquiring layman.

Whatever courses in music the pupils are pursuing in class, or not pursuing, as the case may be, all schools with a strong musical tradition have a wide range of extra-curricular activities. Schools retaining their pupils up to the age of 16 and beyond have been able to develop four-part singing and some, including non-selective schools, have given excellent performances of full-scale oratorios and operas. Such schools, retaining their best instrumentalists beyond the normal school leaving age, have also been able to develop well-balanced orchestras and bands comprising both younger and older pupils. This concentration of effort, by keen and perhaps talented pupils over the entire secondary age-range, is obviously to be encouraged and the way of achieving it is one of the problems that may have to be faced in the future.

Organisation and Staffing

In an educational situation it is always advisable to keep ideal circumstances in mind, however necessary it may be temporarily to accept a compromise. It is useful, therefore, for the headmaster, headmistress or the head of the music department of any school to set down clearly on paper what his objectives would be if given the maximum facilities. Sometimes, in the case of schools in a two or three-tier system, this might mean pooling ideas. Whatever the circumstances, it is important to arrive at a clear idea of what the curriculum, time-table, premises, equipment and so on ought ideally to be, irrespective of any difficulties that might be encountered. Such an exercise may be hypothetical but it has the merit of facing needs, of looking ahead and, perhaps, of suggesting a temporary compromise which might otherwise be overlooked.

The ideal is a large homogeneous music department accommodated in a purpose-built suite of rooms and well-staffed, under a head of department, by a team of full-time and part-time teachers who between them can cover the whole range of the work required. Information about planning new music accommodation (and, by implication, in adapting older premises) is contained in Building Bulletin No. 30, *Secondary School Design: Drama and Music* (HMSO 1966). When planning a new secondary school, it should not be difficult to include suitable accommodation for music along these lines. Schools accommodated in older premises and, perhaps, dispersed over three or four buildings some distance apart have to adapt as best they can. Advice is given in Building Bulletin No. 40: *New Problems in School Design: Comprehensive Schools from Existing Buildings* (HMSO 1968). If possible a music wing should be contrived in one building and as much of the work centred there as difficulties permit. This should certainly include the instrumental teaching, optional courses at the 14–16 and 16–18 levels, and most of the voluntary musical activities.

It is sometimes possible even for pupils doing the basic course to have their music lessons in the music wing if subjects are so grouped in the time-table that a complete day or half-day can be spent in the same building. If music has to be taught in separate buildings, each should have a room that is properly equipped for the work (see Chapter 8).

The quality of staff that can be obtained depends to a considerable extent upon the range of musical activities that are offered. It is particularly important to offer sufficient opportunities, including scope for developing advanced work and corporate activities, to attract a first-rate head of department, who should be something of an impresario as well as a good musician, organiser and teacher. The large maintained secondary school, in fact, needs a head of music who enjoys the same prestige as the director of music in a public school and who also, in order to deal with administration, has at least as much relief from routine class teaching as most teacher-librarians. In order to attract suitable applicants it may be desirable to pool some of the musical work which might normally be done in two or three separate buildings or even in separate schools. For example, one school base, comprising three separate schools each under its own headmaster, has appointed a director of music for the base as a whole, with responsibility for organising instrumental teaching, combined musical activities, recitals by visiting artists and so on, and even for recommending some interchange of staff for normal class teaching between the three schools. A somewhat similar arrangement might be considered for schools in a two-tier system on the same campus. The supporting music staff should have complementary abilities. At least one general music teacher with special experience of instrumental work is desirable in each school, but some visiting instrumental teachers or instructors are also usually required. An eight form-entry comprehensive school with flourishing music would need three full-time teachers plus about half-a-dozen visiting instrumentalists. Valuable assistance with the voluntary activities is also given in many schools by musically gifted members of the staff who are mainly concerned with teaching other subjects.

In schools where, for one reason or another, it is not immediately possible to build up a strong music department, it may be necessary to forgo some of the corporate benefits which large scale musical activities can bring. It is still desirable, however, to provide for the individual needs of those pupils who wish to study music to the limits of their ability and, if those needs cannot be met within the school, further opportunities may be obtained extra-murally. This is where the music centre comes in. In Leicestershire, for example, where for some years past many of the secondary schools have been organised on a two-tier system, an extensive scheme of instrumental work has been built up on a basis of music centres, supplemented by holiday residential courses. Music centres can be of many different kinds and should always be planned to satisfy local needs. They are discussed more fully in the following chapter.

The Basic Course (age 11–14)

It has been said already that the purpose of a basic music course should be to give the ordinary pupil opportunities to make music up to the limit of his capabilities both creatively and re-creatively, to extend his general musical knowledge and to accustom him to the use of musical notation, at least for reference. This applies equally to schools in which the lower forms are streamed, unstreamed or broad-banded. Some basic music courses in the past have been planned with half an eye to the handful of pupils who might subsequently take music in GCE; indeed, textbooks have been published with that objective directly in view. In cannot be stated too strongly that a basic music course should be designed for the benefit of the pupils as a whole without any consideration of subsequent examination requirements, either GCE or CSE. It may be added, also, that if a really interesting basic course is planned it will encourage far more pupils to continue with an optional course, and will indeed prepare them better for it, than has been the general experience with a narrower academic approach in the past.

Ideally the basic course should be a continuation of enterprising work at the primary or middle school level (at whatever age transfer to secondary education may be) and in some areas, through the help of the music adviser, schools' music association or exchanges of visits between the music teachers concerned, excellent continuity is maintained. In this connection it has been found that, where record cards are sent up from the primary school, it is useful to include a note on children's musical ability. However close the liaison there will always have to be some stock-taking when pupils arrive at their secondary school. The teacher will want to know what individual pupils can do; arrangements will have to be made for the instrumentalists amongst them to continue lessons; it might be advisable to find out what songs the pupils already know. In making these preliminary investigations it is much more important, of course, to establish the newcomers' interests than to discover the gaps in their musical knowledge.

A well equipped music room can give new impetus to the sort of music-making the pupils may have experienced already through broadcasts for schools such as *Music Workshop* and *Making Music*. These combined activities, comprising perhaps voices, recorders and simple percussion instruments, can now be extended to include new instruments to which the pupils are introduced in class (guitars, zithers or dulcimers for example) and indeed any other instruments which some of them may be learning out-of-class, such as the clarinet, violin, cornet or piano. Teachers enjoying adequate 'workshop' facilities and having some experience of organising this kind of work find that the pupils normally respond to it with zest and settle down to their various tasks as quickly as they do, say, for art and craft. They also find that they can cope with a wide spread of ability by distributing the various parts according to their different standards of difficulty. An increasing amount of published material for this sort of work is now coming on the market but, other things being equal, it is usually best for the teacher to arrange his own scores, preferably in consultation with the performers concerned. The composition and production of a class opera may offer the most exciting possibilities of all.

Whilst this kind of combined activity can bring the realism of an orchestral or operatic rehearsal into the classroom and commit the pupils to an individual responsibility which was sometimes lacking in traditional music lessons in the past, it does not necessarily follow that, in itself, it is enough. Both boys and girls should still absorb a repertory of songs, they will need more than ever to use musical notation as a visual aid, and they should still acquire some general musical knowledge and learn to form opinions of their own about the music that they hear. Opportunities for all these things may arise incidentally from the combined work that is done and, indeed, opportunities should actually be contrived to arise in this way as far as possible, but the teacher should always keep an eye on the overall progress that is being made and assess it from time to time.

Singing has to be considered from two points of view, repertory and technique. At the secondary stage folk and national songs provide excellent material for the combined activities that have just been described. Art songs, on the other hand, are usually sung only with piano accompaniment. As time puts a limit upon the number of art songs that can be learnt during the basic course, thought is needed in selecting those that merit inclusion in the list (or in the alternative lists which the teacher may draw up to save himself from too much repetition). They should be selected, in the first place, with a view to extending the pupils' musical knowledge rather than to polishing for performance. For example, although they would not attempt it publicly, a mixed form aged 13–14 might tackle Schubert's *Erl King*, splitting into three voices to take the spectre, the father and the child; or a class of boys whose voices were changing might attempt Schumann's *Two Grenadiers* simply to get to know the song, with its famous quotation from *La Marseillaise*. A well-balanced selection of art songs, including arias from oratorio and opera, modern as well as classical, should be learnt in this way with repertory primarily in mind, but each song should also enable the teacher to mention some interesting point about its composer, period or style. If not conflicting with other aims, some of these songs might also be polished and perhaps performed.

Singing technique is something of a misnomer at this stage because, as in the primary school, good singing depends more upon imitating a good model than upon formal voice training. It is noteworthy, indeed, that some of the best singing comes from schools where no systematic vocal or breathing exercises are given. Nevertheless, the ability to sing well, with good tone, intonation, enunciation and phrasing, is something that should be cultivated. Although opinion differs as to methods of voice training for the solo singer, most class teachers favour plenty of humming and quiet, relaxed singing, much of it unaccompanied to develop self reliance and powers of critical listening. Adolescent boys in particular need help and encouragement in stabilising their change of voice within its temporarily restricted compass and in learning to maintain a part and read from the bass clef. Some teachers attempt to satisfy the differing needs of girls and boys at that stage by using S.A.B. arrangements, of which an increasing number are coming into print. Others prefer to separate boys and girls, in which case the girls can often attempt songs of much greater technical difficulty. Indeed, a really good girls' group of this kind can provide great artistic satisfaction and excellent training in the reading and holding of independent parts through the medium of vocal music alone. At this level the acquisition of technique is an investment for the future which the pupils should not be denied, but it is quite unnecessary to separate it from music which is both intrinsically worth while and appropriate to their age. It is not only a question of teaching singing but of guiding taste. For example, if it came to the choice of a song for two-part singing the fine edge of well-edited Henry Purcell might be preferable at this stage to the sentiment of Johann Strauss blurred by re-arrangement and added words.

Musical literacy is a relative term which can mean many things—the ability to write down some new music that has been heard, or to read a part at sight in a madrigal or simply to recognise the opening bars of the National Anthem in print. The important thing to remember in fitting it into the basic course is that it is better to aim for the attainable and succeed than to reach for the unattainable and fail.

There is a well known story that the solo bass of Chester Cathedral choir, confronted with the composer's manuscript of *Why do the nations* with the ink scarcely dry upon it, was able to turn Handel's wrath by pointing out that he could certainly read 'at sight' although not, he regretted, 'at first sight'. This nice distinction is of particular importance in schools, where the use of notation as an aid to memory has sometimes been overlooked in an attempt to achieve a degree of literacy that can only be attained by the very few. Too much attention has sometimes been given to dull sight reading exercises and too little to using notation to overcome difficulties in real music. Notation is particularly useful, for instance, in reminding singers of a slight difference between two otherwise identical phrases. Countless examples could be given from songs in common use in schools and one of the most familiar comes from Schubert's *Hark, hark the lark* where there is often confusion between

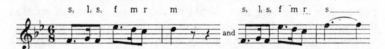

Reference to notation will immediately correct these difficulties of pitch and time-value and will, moreover, help to demonstrate that reading music is a practicable and useful thing to do. Simple instrumental playing as a class activity is obviously a great help in developing reading facility. In singing, the teacher should also ensure that the pupils make quick but frequent reference to printed music in a variety of ways, not least in following the accompaniment as well as the vocal line. The recognition in print of familiar tunes is a useful accomplishment and, over a period of time, the teacher can build up a suitable repertory either on cards or on large manuscript sheets. 'The week's quotations' can be pinned up in this way. The following of scores, simplified or full, also provides good experience in using notation. At first this may amount to no more than silently following

the melody of a song or a single stave score like a First Violin/
Conductor part, but many other variants will readily suggest themselves, such as distributing a set of orchestral parts round the class
before a recording of the work is played. In a lively basic course
there will probably be no place for musical dictation, which tends to
occupy a disproportionate amount of time, nor for verbal note-
taking, even if dignified with the name of 'research'. If any writing
is done it is advisable to confine it to music that the group is to
perform, producing playing parts for example, or to building up an
anthology of tunes.

General Musical Knowledge or Musical Appreciation as terminology
might once have had it, is another aspect of music in which it is
advisable to keep an eye on progress periodically, although it should
never be considered in isolation from the rest of the work. Practical
experience of plenty of good music through the basic course can lead
to wider musical knowledge quite incidentally. As with every other
aspect of the work the resourceful teacher will seize, and indeed
promote, opportunities to make brief, interesting digressions. An
obvious example, but one that may be mentioned because its opportunities are sometimes overlooked, is *The Trout*, which both prompts
comment on Schubert's piano accompaniments and offers an
introduction to chamber music. Links with other subjects, in which
music is particularly rich, are another source of interest.

Music itself is dependent upon science and craft; it is conditioned by
history and geography; it has been inspired by literature and art; the
church, theatre and ballroom have all exerted their influence. There
is, indeed, no limit to interesting observations along these lines. The
more casual these digressions are made to seem the more effective
they can be, but the teacher himself should naturally have some plan
in mind, and should check on how it is progressing from time to time.

The immense impact of television, transistor radio and gramophone
on the young teenager is obviously something to be reckoned with,
both as a help and, some might say, as a handicap. On the one hand
there is a new wealth of musical experience on which the teacher can
draw to supplement his work in class; opera, ballet, symphony
orchestra and the like are no longer confined to the theatre and the
concert hall but are now accessible to all. On the other hand there is
the inescapable, pervasive influence of pop. The high and low brow
products of mass communication need not necessarily conflict,
indeed the main thing to establish in the pupils' eyes is that they can
live happily side by side.

This does not mean that the teacher should lower his standards of
taste: young people do not expect their teachers to be pop fans. They
are very responsive, however, to friendly interest in what is currently

popular in 'their world', especially if it is backed up by a few pertinent comments which show that the teacher has paid them the compliment of finding out something about the music they listen to in their leisure hours. Once this sort of mutual respect has been established the teacher is well placed for extending their interests over part at least of the vast territory that exists between the beat group and the string quartet. The scoring of theme music associated with well-known broadcast programmes, the characteristic flavour of the orchestral background to western films, the technical accomplishment of popular instrumentalists, the simple form of many popular songs, writing topical verses to fit traditional tunes, the musicianship required to be a good musical comedian, jazz-vocalising Bach, Tippett's use of negro spirituals; almost anything interesting, in fact, that starts within the sight of the popular camp and leads to something as yet unseen. If he will come to terms with it and use it in this way, the teacher will find that mass communication is far less of a hindrance than a help.

Enough has already been said to show that the basic course should be planned as a whole and should, above all, offer absorbing practical experience. In the past the different elements of 'singing', 'theory' and 'appreciation' were sometimes considered, and even time-tabled, as separate subjects of study. This arose, no doubt, from a belief that the criterion of success lay in how much the pupils had learnt academically about music and, perhaps, demonstrated through tests of various kinds. A more revealing criterion nowadays is how much they want to go on making music at the end of their basic course.

The Optional Course (age 14–16)

The purpose of an optional course, as has just been suggested, should be to enable pupils to go on experiencing music. It is not necessary for them to work towards an examination, although some of them may wish to do so, indeed, it is best to devise a course without external pressures of this kind.

A fundamental requirement is that the course should have adequate numbers. This is not just a question of economy in staffing. In music it is necessary to have a group large enough to form workable vocal and instrumental ensembles. A group of less than about a dozen is limited in the range of work which it can undertake and may suffer some loss of interest in consequence; about twenty, as for some other practical subjects, is probably the ideal size. It is desirable therefore, that as many pupils as possible should have the opportunity of opting for music and that the two extremes of the ability range should not be excluded, as sometimes happens. If two groups are formed, as may be necessary in large schools, it is useful if they coincide in the time-table once or twice a week, so that they can combine for larger activities at the teachers' discretion. Other requirements are adequate time and facilities. Generally speaking optional music needs about the same amount of time as a modern language course (four or five periods a week), whilst good 'workshop' provision is even more necessary at this stage than it is in the basic course. It is particularly helpful to have a few instrumental rooms for work in smaller groups; where these are lacking, temporary alternatives can sometimes be found.

The content of the course should naturally be adapted to the needs of those who are taking it. Some pupils in the lower academic streams are good at music and can hold their own with the best; on the other hand, some who are keen to do music are comparatively slow. As in the basic course, however, it is possible to cope with a fairly wide range of ability in practical work; in choral singing the quicker readers can help the slower, whilst in orchestral playing parts can be allotted according to their difficulty. Music-making in smaller ensembles should form an important part of the course and these can usually be adapted to suit the personnel—madrigals, guitar, brass or recorder groups, string and woodwind ensembles, indeed almost anything that extends the pupil's experience and makes realistic use of the instrumental skill which, it may be hoped, most of them will acquire from instrumental tuition provided alongside the optional course (see Voluntary Activities below). This ensemble work need not be technically difficult but, at whatever level it is attempted, it should always be artistically well done. In addition to music-making, a great deal of flexibility can also be achieved by encouraging individual pupils to pursue some musical interest of their own. Here again the field is almost limitless—individual performance, making an instrument, composition or arranging, a well illustrated paper or lecture on some musical topic to mention just a few possibilities—and the teacher need only ensure that it leads to some original effort and involves something more than collecting pictures or copying from a book.

Whilst corporate music-making and individual interests may occupy a good proportion of the time, it is also necessary to develop pupils' musical literacy up to the limit of their ability and to extend their general musical knowledge. In considering literacy it is necessary as in the basic course, to put first things first. Generally speaking it is more important to read than to write. Realistic practice in music reading should therefore take precedence over dictation, which is not so much a method of training as a method of testing used in written examinations. There is no point in giving written dictation until the pupils have acquired considerable facility in practical skills such as singing the solfa syllables to well-known tunes by ear or echoing simple phrases on an instrument, an exercise in which pupils can work in pairs. Similarly, there is no point in introducing written harmony until, through part-singing and the use of instruments such as the chordal dulcimer, auto-harp or guitar (or the piano for capable pianists), the pupils have acquired a working knowledge of the basic chords and can use them with confidence in a practical way. Confidence in playing simple music by ear is, in fact, a perfectly justifiable and valuable end in itself, as well as being an essential prelude to successful written work.

Although the instructional value of ear tests of the traditional kind is questionable, it is still desirable to develop an analytical ear. As far as possible, this should be related to the requirements of actual performance. The player or singer needs to be aware of what is going on in the performance as a whole, the phrasing, instrumentation, dynamics, changes of tempo and so on. Ideally he should develop this awareness with every piece that he performs, but it is sometimes useful to aid his concentration by giving him something more tangible to do. Simple score-annotating provides valuable training of this kind and the filling in of a skeleton score (say of a Haydn minuet) has the added advantage of being a flexible and useful exercise for pupils of all levels of ability within the group.

The surest way of extending the pupils' general musical knowledge is to encourage them to extend it themselves. Every opportunity should be taken (by displaying programmes, for example) to interest them in music which they can hear out of class, on television, on sound radio or in the concert hall, to get them to discuss it next day in school and to make scores and books available so that they can follow up points of interest on their own. More specific guidance may also be desirable in class. This should be considerably broader in its scope than the detailed analysis of one or two set works that has been prescribed for some examinations at the 14–16 level in the past; on the other hand it should not be so broad as to become superficial and unrelated to practical experience. Within these limits there are many fruitful lines of approach—studying one period of music, learning certain outstanding works representative of several periods, following the development of a particular aspect of music, basing the working upon individual projects and so on—and it does not much matter which method the teacher selects as long as it is constantly illuminated with musical examples and arouses the pupil's interest and a desire to find out more for himself.

Examinations may be a desirable conclusion to the optional course, at any rate for some pupils. A small minority of these pupils, hoping to go on from 'A' levels to a university, college of music or college of education, and having the ability to do so whilst continuing plenty of practical music-making, might find 'O' level GCE a good stepping-stone. But they might well find CSE an equally good preparation for 'A' level and, for most of the pupils, this would almost certainly be a more suitable examination to take. In this connection it should be emphasised that schools are entitled to put up their own syllabuses, for GCE as well as for CSE and are, indeed, encouraged to do so. A full description of an experimental examination in music for CSE is given in *Examination Bulletin No.* 10 (HMSO 1966).

Work at the 16–18 Level

A number of music centres established in colleges of technology and of further education in different parts of the country provide training for students in the 16–18 age range. The success of these centres arises partly from the fact that some young people prefer to leave school at 16 and continue their education elsewhere, but also from the inability of many schools to provide for the needs of promising young musicians of that age. Schools cannot be expected in all circumstances to provide facilities of this kind. They should decide quite clearly, however, whether they can or cannot do so adequately and, if they decide to shoulder the responsibility themselves rather than recommend their pupils to seek further training elsewhere, they should ensure that they fulfill it satisfactorily.

Pupils with academic ability who have obtained good results at 'O' level and have a reasonable chance of obtaining two or three 'A' levels, of which music might be one, create no problems. They fit into the normal pattern of sixth form work easily enough and, even though they may be few in numbers and are consequently rather expensive in staffing, there are few schools which do not manage to provide for them in one way or another, as they do for advanced students of the less common languages.

The real problem is to cater for pupils who have sufficient practical ability in music to warrant continued study but who still need to obtain some more 'O' levels to qualify for further education. The need for courses of this kind can be gauged from the fact that, over a ten year period, one music centre in the north of England sent well over 100 such pupils, mainly from non-selective schools, to colleges of education, colleges of music and even to universities. And the need will obviously grow with increasingly effective optional courses at the 14–16 level. Few, if any, of these pupils need aim for 'A' level, even in music, although they might well overlap with candidates taking 'A' level music for part of their work. They should reach a high standard of instrumental playing, however, perhaps taking the graded examinations of one of the recognised music examining boards, and they should also develop skill and confidence in choral singing, chamber music playing and keyboard harmony, as well as extending their musical literacy and general musical knowledge. It would not be unreasonable to expect a major study of this kind to occupy about a third of their time, the rest being taken up by continuing their general education. Such pupils would, in effect, be members of a non-academic sixth form.

The more effective that optional music courses at the 14–16 and the 16–18 levels become, the less necessary will it be to provide short intensive courses in music for those who have decided to take up primary school teaching as a career, such as some schools, and particularly girls' schools, have provided in the past. Nevertheless this is a need that should be kept in mind and met if necessary The best kind of preparation for these latecomers to music is to develop their musical literacy through singing and simple instrumental playing on lines similar to those outlined for the optional course at the 14–16 level.

Apart from pupils who are studying music in the hope of continuing it in one way or another as a practical activity after leaving school, it is necessary to consider those who may have done no formal musical work since the age of 14. In some schools where minority time has been allotted to music in the sixth form it has been used to provide a veneer of musical knowledge with a view to answering questions in the G.C.E. General Paper. Thumb-nail history of this kind rarely does much good, but there is no doubt that the interest of many pupils is aroused to music in their later teens and that they want to find out more about it. A wide and challenging range of opportunity is open to the teacher in catering for this need and one of his objectives will be to prompt pupils to take an active part in music through voluntary activities of various kinds. His main objective will be to devise a course in music for the non-musician in much the same way as his science colleagues devise a course in science for the non-scientist.

In the latter case there is usually insufficient time to teach the non-scientists science but enough to show them how science works. Much the same goes for music. Score-following makes a good beginning which calls for little previous knowledge but fully engages the pupils' attention and prompts many questions and explanations. Links with other studies in the arts, sciences or humanities are also fruitful points from which interest may grow, as are modern developments such as electronic music. The range of choice, indeed, is almost limitless and it need only be added that, although the passive lecture method may sometimes have a place, it is usually best to plan the work so that the pupils, in some way, are actively engaged.

Voluntary Activities

Amongst the many voluntary activities that should emanate from a flourishing music department instrumental playing may be mentioned

5

Music Schools

Choir Schools

Reference has already been made at the beginning of Chapter 1 to the schools that were a feature of the monastic system of the middle ages. These are the earliest examples of a tradition which has been continued down the centuries in an almost unbroken line, and which still flourishes in the choir schools of the present day. Although these schools exist for the primary purpose of training choristers, they cater also for the general education of their pupils, whether choristers or not, and they have shown that the highest standards of academic attainment can be achieved despite the fact that a large part of a pupil's time is spent in striving towards excellence in a comparatively narrow field. A brief description of these traditional schools may thus be relevant.

Seven of the thirty-five schools which comprise the Choir Schools Association cater for choristers only and vary in size from about 16 to 60 pupils. The remainder are mainly larger schools which include other pupils and in which the choristers may form only a small proportion of the total numbers. Whatever the school, the choristers spend an average of about two hours a day—sometimes more—in rehearsal and in the singing of the daily offices and the Sunday services. Occasional special services make further claims on their time. In addition, virtually every chorister learns an instrument and many of them learn two, so that the total time devoted to musical activities is considerable. In the schools catering for choristers only, time-tabling is comparatively simple; in the larger schools the special duties of the chorister minority have to be fitted in to a time-table geared in large measure to the needs of the non-choristers. On the other hand problems concerning finance, staffing and organisation of team games are more acute in the smaller schools than in the larger. Individual schools cope with their problems in their own ways, and by and large the cathedral chorister follows the same academic curriculum as the ordinary preparatory-school boy, keeping pace with him and indeed sometimes outstripping him.

The musical training of a chorister encourages poise, self-reliance, a feeling of personal responsibility and a highly developed sense of team work. He is often called upon to organise his work and his leisure time in a way which boys and girls normally experience only when they go to a university. He is set a standard of quality and personal effort by doing one thing supremely well. And he is engaged in an exacting artistic activity which, like the practice of all the arts, stimulates liveliness of mind.

Schools with a Music Bias

The strong musical bias found in the choir schools has little counterpart as yet in schools at large, although a few of the maintained schools, and many more of the independent ones, provide opportunities for individual pupils to devote a large part of their time to music. To give two examples, a few years ago the headmistress of a maintained grammar school near London took it upon herself to arrange half-time schooling for a girl who is now a well-known solo violinist, so that she could practise several hours a day and still continue her general education far enough to matriculate; and one large county borough in the north of England has produced several outstanding young musicians who have remained at school with a reduced timetable up to sixth form level. Some authorities are now looking beyond individual arrangements of this kind and are considering the provision of at least one school in their area with a music bias built into the curriculum. It may be of interest to describe the proposal for one such school, although it has not yet been built.

This school, in Manchester, is to be a four-form-entry replacement of the present High School of Art and will include a one-form-entry of pupils wishing to study music as an important part of their general education, on lines parallel with the present art-biased courses which have been running successfully for several years and on which a great deal of useful experience has been gained. The intention of the art courses has not been to produce professional artists, although some pupils do take up art as a career, but to make use of art as a valuable educational medium in itself, in conjunction with general education of a more traditional kind. The pupils in the music stream will do some art, just as the art streams at present take some music, but they will also spend about two periods a day on their special music course and, like the artists, a good deal of their work will be done individually or in small groups. Unlike the artists, however, who can work together individually in a large studio, much of their music time will have to be spent in practising alone. This has necessitated planning for an unusually large number of small instrumental rooms, as may be seen from the schedule of accommodation, (which is reproduced in Chapter 8 by kind permission of the Manchester Local Education Authority).

Schools for Highly-Talented Musical Children

When Joachim was interviewed for entry to the Leipzig Conservatoire at the age of eleven, having lived and worked with Joseph Boehm in his household for the previous two years, Mendelssohn reported that he required no further lessons in violin playing but that he should extend his general education. No doubt it was Mendelssohn's wise decision at that time that gave Joachim the intellectual stature to rise above mere virtuosity and to dominate the violin playing and the chamber music of Europe for half a century, and nobody today would deny the importance of a good general education in the upbringing of a highly musical child. The only problem is when and how it should be given.

On the Continent it used to be the custom to train musicians first and educate them afterwards. In this country we have tended to educate them first and to trust, perhaps with undue optimism, that genuine talent will have the strength to emerge. For a child of moderate musical ability who may become a keen amateur musician or even embark upon a successful if not a spectacular career as a professional player or as a teacher of music, this policy is eminently sensible, especially if more provision is made for general education courses with a music bias on the lines that have just been described. Genius, however, is a law unto itself and does not take kindly to education organised on normal lines, however sensible those may be. In other sectors of the educational system, for those who are physically handicapped, mentally defective or socially delinquent, it is widely recognised that special provision has to be made, sometimes at very considerable cost. Genius, a less common phenomenon, is equally deserving of special treatment. Various arguments have been advanced in recent years by eminent musicians to support this view. There is the international one that this country starts training its highly talented musicians too late to enable them to compete on equal terms with young virtuosos trained under more selective conditions abroad. There is also the national one, that we are not producing enough good professional musicians, particularly string players, to maintain the corps of performers at a level to supply increasing demand. But perhaps the strongest argument, arising from our widely accepted belief that education should be geared to the age, aptitude and ability of the individual child, is that exceptional ability bordering on genius, although it may be rare, is something to be reckoned with for the sake of the child himself, in the same way as some other recognised divergence from the norm, and that to fail to give genius its opportunity may be as inhumane as to ignore the requirements of a child who is actually handicapped in some way. There is no aspect of education in which this problem occurs more forcibly than it does in music. Obviously there is no simple solution. Special state music schools of the kind that exist in Russia, Hungary and elsewhere would not fit readily into the established pattern in this country, where maintained schools are in the charge of local education authorities, but the two or three small schools for young musicians that have been started here independently (especially the Menuhin School at Stoke D'Abernon) have pointed towards lines of development for the future. This is not the place to discuss in detail what has been achieved already or what form future developments might take. These are still matters for more general discussion and experiment, in which it may be hoped that local authorities as well as independent educationists will take part. The local authorities are the only bodies able to finance highly musical children whose education is not paid for privately or through some charitable trust. Any school for such children which hopes to enlist public support should therefore be acceptable to local authorities both on educational and financial grounds. This does not mean that it need follow any orthodox pattern, but simply that it should be seen to provide reasonably well for the education of the whole child and, in cost, should compare reasonably well with other forms of special education. Although no solution can be offered, a few comments may usefully be made on the problem as a whole and on the needs of highly talented children in particular.

The most important consideration is to develop a child's imagination and originality, since it is these qualities more than any others that carry an artist to the heights. Perceptive teaching and the chance of hearing great singers and players periodically are obvious essentials. The opportunity to play and exchange ideas with other talented children is also a powerful stimulus. It follows, therefore, that a school for such children should be large enough to provide a reasonable range of musical activities, and that it should be easily accessible to and from a centre where outstanding performers and teachers of the highest quality could be found. It may be assumed, also, that it should be open to both boys and girls, of any race or creed, and that some boarding facilities would probably be necessary. From the musical point of view the age-range of the pupils need not, indeed it could not, be confined to the normal pattern of primary and secondary education. Some pupils would certainly be ready for such a school by the age of 8 or 9 years and some might wish to stay on until 16 or even 18. Musically, this would not matter. One of the great charms of music is that musicians of widely different ages, children as well as adults, can work together on an equal and mutually advantageous footing. Nevertheless a wide age-range creates other problems, which have to be surmounted. One possibility is that the small music school might work in association with some larger school that offered a wider range of educational opportunity and that was, at the same time, willing to adapt itself to the special needs of these highly talented young musicians.

The selection of pupils for such a school creates a problem of its own. No local education authority, however large, is likely to produce enough musical prodigies for its officers to build up much experience of assessing them. Serious consideration should always be given, however, to the needs of any child who stands out noticeably above the general run of child musicians and further guidance, if necessary, should be obtained. The principals of any of the major colleges of music, calling upon the experience of appropriate members of their staff, would certainly be glad to help.

Music Centres

Although music centres cater for a less specialised kind of musical education than is required for highly talented children, they are becoming an increasingly necessary adjunct to normal work in schools. An indication of the present distribution of the larger centres in England and Wales is given in a recent report, *Music Centres* (Standing Conference for Amateur Music, 1966), which also contains advice on organisation and staffing. For present purposes a wider definition may be adopted than the one used in that report and a music centre may be taken to include almost any centralised arrangement for tuition, study or performance. Some authorities have been able to set up a fully operational centre rapidly in a disused school building, but at its simplest a centre may comprise no more than a few instrumental classes on Saturday mornings, accommodated in some convenient school.

Many authorities have made arrangements of this kind, which obviously have a lot to commend them on the grounds of economical use of staff and equipment, concentration of ability and also (since there is no reason why they should be confined either to the primary or secondary levels) continuity of instruction. Further developments might be to arrange for instruction during school hours or to cater for some of the more specialised needs of music which cannot be met adequately in individual schools, particularly advanced work at the 16–18 level. The centre might also work in association with the Liberal Studies Department of a college of technology. Music centres, of course, should be planned to meet local needs, and the probable need for future expansion should be kept in mind. The rapid growth in the number of music centres of all kinds in England and Wales gives some indication of the increasingly important part which they will play in musical education in the future. Not the least of their virtues is that they give children the personal interest of a small group of teachers who can follow their progress right through from primary to further education. They also give them a material place in an adult music organisation, an organisation whose mere existence contributes much to the standing and prestige of music-making within the community.

6

Special Schools

Value of Music

The value of music in the personal development and social experience of children in need of special education cannot be overstressed. It is one of the few subjects, interests or skills which can develop steadily from early childhood to adulthood and so help the adult towards social integration. It can stimulate a vivid response and so generate mental vigour which will carry over to other work. It can make an immediate appeal without the struggle to recover or acquire techniques lost through interrupted schooling, and can thus be presented at the level of the children's chronological or mental age.

It can bring a sense of achievement in practical music-making through which nervous and badly co-ordinated children gain poise and confidence. For those in residential or hospital schools, it can provide a link with the outside world, while for those whose handicap is grave and permanent, it may help to compensate for things that will never lie within their scope or power. Indirectly it can help children with special intellectual handicaps to communicate in a very positive way through movement. In dance, where their body is the instrument, the use of music as a stimulus for movement is of the utmost importance. Careful selection of short pieces of music, containing clearly marked phrases of contrasting character can greatly assist the children in the ordering of their action. Their movement response to music may well be unpredictable, sometimes violent, but the opportunities that are offered for the release of emotional tension, and the development of relationships with others around them, can be of considerable benefit to children who are emotionally disturbed or who have only limited academic ability.

Although more experience and knowledge of how to teach music is needed in many spheres of special education, a great deal of valuable research has been done in the past ten years by bodies such as the Standing Conference for Amateur Music, the Schools' Music Association, and the Central Council for the Disabled, as well as by individual teachers working in schools, colleges and universities. Some

51

authoritative books have also been published on particular aspects of the work. Any teacher seeking specialist guidance of this kind should obviously consult one of these sources or attend an appropriate course. The following notes are intended only as a general guide.

General Organisation

What can be attempted depends on the nature of the child's disability and on the type of school and its organisation. Handicapped pupils placed in primary and secondary schools can take part in most of the normal musical work. Much the same work can be undertaken in special schools, although it is sometimes hampered by problems of organisation and the lack of specialist teaching. The presence of one gifted musician on the staff can do much to help other teachers who teach some music. A visiting musician experienced in special education can do much the same. The problems facing the teacher are many. Frequently the age range of a class is wide, the school population may be so fluctuating that much of the work has to be planned for short periods of schooling and, because the number of contributory schools may be legion and many children will have suffered from broken schooling, the co-ordination of previous experience and the finding of a common core of knowledge may be well-nigh impossible. It is essential, however, that all children should at least be given opportunities for musical experience.

In many of these schools a fairly wide range of work, including singing, instrumental playing, listening, aural training and music reading, may be undertaken; and in some of them, movement and drama with music may play a useful role. Singing gives all pupils opportunities for taking an active part in music. The great variety of traditional music of this and other countries, especially of songs with choruses and cumulative songs, will prove invaluable. Classical and modern songs also may be taught. Because the physical weaknesses of some of the children may preclude the development of good vocal tone, the choice of song should be governed by the imaginative experiences offered, so that whatever technical imperfections may have to be accepted, good interpretation and a feeling for style and phrasing will give the children the satisfaction of taking part in an artistic performance. The provision of copies of song books, light in weight and convenient to hold, and of sheet music is important, as learning to follow and recognise the rhythmic pattern and melodic outline of the tunes is an essential step to a more precise study of music reading. The approach to notation, and the development of aural training, music reading and writing depend very much on the musical ability of the teacher. Where a competent musician is available, a good deal of such work, much of it individual according to the age and ability of the child, can be done.

Infants' school—music corner

Younger juniors sing and play to guitar accompaniment

Practical composition

Movement with music

Primary school string orchestra

Music class at the 'Yehudi Menuhin School'

Secondary school music club

Opposite: Making music by sound and touch

Instrument technicians at work

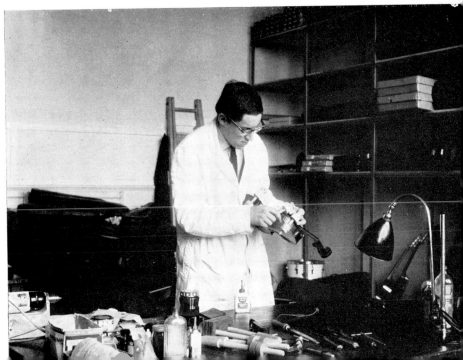

Brass band festival

Interesting experiments with simple instruments, making up tunes to sing or play on pipe or recorder with, for some, an attendant interest in music writing, scoring pieces for percussion playing, and learning to follow an orchestral score, are all possible. Instrumental work may begin with simple melodic instruments and may develop in a number of ways, including the playing of orchestral instruments, according to the type of school and the child's capabilities. In some residential special schools good orchestras have developed. Frequent opportunities for listening to music should be given by means of broadcasting, gramophone records and, best of all, live performances by visiting artists, by teachers and by instrumentalists from neighbouring schools. The needs of special schools should always be kept in mind when planning concerts for schools or the programme of peripatetic instrumental teachers.

Schools for Delicate and Physically Handicapped Children

In schools for the delicate and physically handicapped all the work outlined can be attempted. Any class, however, may contain children who will stay only for a short time, as well as those who will remain for a long period. A number of these pupils may suffer from respiratory diseases.

The population of schools catering for the severely disabled and otherwise physically handicapped will, on the whole, be more stable, so that a progressive course can be planned. For these pupils music may become one of their greatest and most easily available pleasures. Where it is possible the teaching of a musical instrument is to be encouraged, and the provision of peripatetic teaching is often desirable. In view of the valuable contribution it can make to a physically handicapped child who has musical gifts, it should be considered as part of the curriculum for those who could profit by it. In all the schools for epileptics in this country, class singing is taught, while in some schools instrumental tuition and orchestral playing have been successfully introduced. It has been found that music, particularly instrumental work, together with movement and dancing, can be wholly absorbing, and so, in common with other activities which fully engage the children's interests, can contribute notably to their well-being. Many children suffering from cerebral palsy have difficulty in using their hands, so ways of playing instruments with the feet, arm or body have to be devised.

Schools for Children with Impaired Hearing

In schools for children whose hearing is impaired, music is introduced as a means of self-expression, through singing and dancing and also as part of the general auditory training. Enunciation of words in singing, particularly with the younger pupils, is frequently far clearer

than in speech, so that singing can make a valuable contribution to
their speech training in general. Melodic training should always be
attempted but it may be found that some children have little sense of
pitch. These children, however, can sometimes sing on a monotone,
and even some who are totally deaf often have considerable powers of
perception of rhythm, and dancing can become a regular part of
their time-table. Percussion instruments are used not only in music
lessons but also as an aid to the development of rhythmical speech,
particularly in helping to overcome the problem of syllabic speech.

Schools for the Blind

Music has always played a large part in the education of the blind.
It is not that the proportion of blind children who show musical
ability is any higher than that of sighted children, but that it is the
only one of the fine arts which can make exactly the same appeal to
the blind as to the sighted and any innate artistic sense is therefore
likely to find this outlet. Doubtless also, the development of the
faculty of hearing and powers of memorisation to compensate for
the loss of sight, which many blind children show so markedly,
draws them towards the art of sound. To achieve success, equal to
that of the sighted, in one of the normal activities of mankind is of
very real psychological value to the handicapped, and music would
be worth its place in the education of the blind for that reason alone.

Most schools very rightly set themselves the task of providing
individual tuition in music for as many children as may desire it.
This is largely in the form of pianoforte lessons; understandably so,
since performance on a keyboard instrument is complete in itself and
gives a desirable sense of independent achievement. It is also the
most suitable instrument for those blind children, and they are many,
who find in the actual physical manipulation of the keyboard an
outlet for the activity of hand and finger which in so many other
ways is denied them. However, there has been a striking growth in
recent years of other instrumental teaching, both string and wind,
which has proved its musical and social value completely, and which
it is hoped will become general in schools for the blind.

In the organisation of class work, it has to be remembered that these
schools are not large and that forms are small. To provide classes of a
suitable size for singing it is often considered advisable to group two
or more forms together; this should be looked upon as a necessary
evil rather than as a positive good, and kept to the minimum in the
interests of suiting the song repertoire to the age of the children. For
all other music classes, the form unit is the best size. This enables the
planning of a properly graded course in general musicianship
through music and movement (most valuable at the infant and junior

stages), percussion, recorders, ear training and listening; Braille musical notation, much more easily grasped when learnt in connection with an instrument than with the voice, may be introduced into the music class as soon as the children have sufficient skill in reading ordinary Braille, generally not younger than 9 or 10. In some cases children can read a Braille score with one hand and play a simple instrument with the other.

Apart from these observations, there is little that was said in Chapters 2 and 3 that does not apply equally to schools for the blind. As boarding schools they have ample opportunity for the development of out-of-school activities; the secondary departments, keeping pupils till 16 years of age, can achieve part-singing with changed voices more successfully than many of their sighted counterparts, and in those places where a training department is under the same roof the choral work can be quite outstanding. Recent developments in string and wind playing also hold out exciting possibilities for the future.

Schools for the Partially Sighted

The problem of those who teach partially sighted children is that of a modification of sighted methods rather than of those used in teaching the blind. Braille is not used as an educational medium. A knowledge of staff notation can and should be taught, but the extent to which music can be read from the staff at the moment of performance, vocal or instrumental, will vary from child to child. Scores in large type can help considerably but good light is essential. Many of the principles of teaching other subjects to the partially sighted are applicable to music, and a resourceful teacher can find many useful analogies to help him.

Hospital Schools

Here, even more than in other special schools, the lack of homogeneity in age and experience has to be reckoned with. In some hospital schools children may be grouped according to age but, in others, grouping according to medical needs may extend the age range from that of pre-school age to adult years. Moreover, the music teacher must accept the many interruptions for medical and nursing attention, which are the main reasons for pupils being in hospital. Further, there is the material difficulty of working in a long ward where it is almost impossible to find a focal point to which the children's attention may be drawn. It is not easy to give pupils a sense of ensemble in singing as children in bed are apt to feel they are singing alone. In some hospitals, beds may be wheeled close to each other, but where this is not permitted the few patients who are mobile may sit between beds or form a small choir or nucleus of tone at the focal teaching point. Where song accompaniments can be provided by the teacher on the guitar, for example, or by players in the ward on simple melodic and percussion instruments, additional interest is brought to choral work. Apart from this, the provision of a piano is desirable for ward teaching. If it is not to prove a barrier between teacher and children, it should be low-backed. A portable electronic keyboard is another possibility.

Percussion playing may be the only instrumental work possible for some patients. Very small children whose only physical activity in their hospital cots is the use of their arms show a highly developed rhythmic response to music through percussion playing, while older pupils who are lying in such positions as to make any music reading or other instrumental playing out of the question, are able to join in both by making suggestions for scoring and by playing in an ensemble which may include percussion, pipes or recorders and voices. Players of recorders or pipes quickly gain facility in reading music and experience much satisfaction from ensemble playing with occupants of neighbouring beds, or with other children who are mobile. The introduction of these instruments also gives pupils pleasure outside lesson hours, as they are able to practice and play together during their leisure time. Where these opportunities are given, pupils will make tremendous efforts to play despite the fact that some of those in orthopaedic wards or hospitals may be confined to positions in which playing any instrument might appear almost impossible. Once a child is sufficiently recovered to take lessons in the school-room, it is possible for anyone who has learned to play an instrument before entering hospital to practise and perhaps to have some instruction. Special arrangements may have to be made for the secondary school pupils who have been preparing before admission to offer music as a subject for GCE or CSE.

Bringing together all pupils who can be moved into a central meeting place provides both a stimulus to music making and the satisfaction of communal musical performance otherwise denied the child in hospital. The value of such occasions both musically and in other ways cannot be over estimated.

Schools for Maladjusted Pupils

Music, including movement response to music, can be of particular help to maladjusted children, who frequently gain in emotional stability through listening to music or taking part in active music making. A Report on Music in Special Schools, published by the Schools Music Association, includes some striking examples of improvements of this kind, quoted by teachers of maladjusted pupils. Although most of these schools are quite small, even in comparison with other special schools, the range of musical experience should be as wide as possible and might include most of the activities already described.

Schools for Educationally Sub-normal Pupils

Among the many difficulties facing the teacher of the educationally sub-normal are the children's limited span of attention, their slow assimilation, their poor retention and, for many, their inability to read words fluently or, in a few cases, at all. Nevertheless many dull children experience emotional satisfaction from their musical activities, whilst some show markedly improved imagination, concentration and poise. Many also develop their social sense as members of a music-making group. With some of these pupils a sense of pitch and of rhythm is slow to develop; others possess as much ability as a normal child, while some are gifted with lovely voices. Every opportunity to develop such talent should be given, since educationally sub-normal children will, by the exercise of what they can do well, become so much the more stable and confident. For such children, music is not so much a subject to be taught as a field to be explored, as an aid to growth of personality.

Songs should be chosen for their imaginative quality; apart from narrative songs where all verses are essential, they should be short and varied in mood. Some of them at least should have links with everyday life. Songs with refrains and cumulative songs should be included, and where a class has sufficient ability, some classical and modern songs can be introduced. Interpretation should be the principal aim in performance; good tone quality and other techniques will probably be subsidiary and may be later developing. Some knowledge of notation can be taught to a number of these pupils, many of whom can read rhythm fluently. Some are able to make headway with pitch reading and where this has been associated with learning a recorder or a bamboo pipe, progress, though slow, has been maintained. Individual improvisation, either with percussion or pitch instruments, provides a valuable direct musical experience which need not be related to notation but which can provide an incentive to learning musical symbols. The value to the educationally sub-normal child of movement to music is considerable and often arises spontaneously from short periods of listening without movement. The intergration of musical activities with dramatic work frequently produces happy results. Visiting artists can provide great stimulus, especially with the use of simple instruments or voices and with understanding presentation. Good visual aids and visits to museums to see old instruments, folk costumes and so on can also stimulate imagination.

7

The Teacher

Attributes

All good music teachers are fascinated by music and have the capacity to make it live. Not all of them are particularly knowledgeable musicians or even capable instrumentalists, but all of them need live music as part of everyday life and, through constant association with it, have developed a lively sense of performance. Many other factors contribute to the successful teacher in the spheres of personality, pedagogics and musical skill, and they are found in an infinite variety of different proportions amongst music teachers as a whole, strength in one factor often helping to balance weakness in another, but the two factors common to all and without which no teacher can excel are delight in music and a sense of style.

The sense of style that enables an infant teacher to vitalise a nursery song and a great conductor to reveal a symphony is essentially the same and it differs not in kind but only in degree. It springs from the fact that music is an art that unfolds itself in time and that, to recreate it, the musician must have a vivid sense of rhythm, of timing and of emphasis. One great conductor claims to rehearse an orchestra with a vocabulary of six words – *Faster – Slower – Longer – Shorter – Louder – Softer*, and, although that may be understatement of the Olympian kind, it nevertheless contains a great deal of fundamental truth. Even the simplest nursery song requires a pliable rhythm that moves forward at one point and holds back at another; it needs a significant pause here or a sense of urgency there; it calls for one word to be loudly declaimed and another to be whispered. The successful folk-singer, although he may not analyse it, has all this in his very bones.

To some extent this sense of style is inborn, in much the same way as, in the visual arts, some people are gifted with a better sense of shape or colour than others, but there is no doubt that, with practice, even quite modest gifts in this direction are capable of great development. The main problem in training, therefore, is to give adequate scope for the development of this sense of style, which can only come from a great deal of informal music-making, whilst at the same time building an adequate foundation of pedagogics and musical skill.

Musical Education at School

Future music teachers are bred in the schools and it is the collective responsibility of the schools, far more than of the universities or colleges of education, to ensure that they produce enough music teachers for their requirements and of the kind they want. At present many students, though interested in music, are reluctant to take it as a main or even as a subsidiary subject in their college of education course because they lack an adequate foundation of musical skill upon which to build. Instead they select some other subject in which they have had a better grounding at school or one in which they believe they have a better chance of reaching an acceptable standard without much previous knowledge. The total number of music students, in fact, is related not only to their interest in the subject but, even more, to the degree of confidence with which they can embark on a music course. This confidence depends upon the background of musical training they have received at school. A good many schools, especially girls' schools, provide a course in general musicianship for potential teachers in the sixth form and, by this means, have undoubtedly encouraged a number of students to take music who might not otherwise have done so. Such courses are a great deal better than nothing, but the only way of substantially improving the present position is to develop optional music courses following on from strong basic courses at the bottom of the school. Students with a background such as this, with systematic instruction in instrumental playing and regular opportunities for exercising musical initiative extending over several years, should be able to look forward to continuing their music at college not only with pleasure but with every confidence of success.

Although the secondary schools thus bear much of the responsibility for producing future music teachers, a good deal also depends upon the kind of training offered in the primary school. It is here that children's attitude to music is implanted and the foundations of their musical skills are laid. The primary school which a student attended as a child may also be the most important factor in leading him to decide whether or not music is a rewarding subject to teach. Whether at the primary or the secondary stage, the artistic quality of his work in school has a direct bearing upon a student's delight in music and upon the development of his sense of style.

Training at College or University

It is beyond the scope of this pamphlet to discuss in detail the training of music teachers. That is the responsibility of the colleges of music, the colleges of education, the area training organisations and universities and of some colleges of further education. The purpose of this section is not to usurp the functions of these bodies but simply to relate the question of training teachers to the main theme of this pamphlet, music in schools, and to discuss a little more fully the over-riding problem that was posed at the end of the section on Attributes.

It has been emphasised already that music in schools should be a living art and that its most successful exponents are artists at whatever level thay may work. Obviously they must also have some technical competence and knowledge of how to teach. In theory, the problem is simply to balance the claims of artistry against those of musical skill and pedagogics. In practice, it is a far from simple problem to solve, indeed, since it is concerned with individuals, it calls ideally for as many solutions as there are music students in training. The problem really revolves round 'balance'. To take a practical example with which the headmistresses of countless infant schools throughout the country are familiar, there is on the one hand the teacher who cannot play an instrument but who can present a song unaccompanied with a vivid sense of style and, on the other, the pianist whose conception of music is wooden but who can just manage to accompany the morning hymn.

From the musical point of view there is no doubt which is preferable. Whilst allowing for individual differences there is no doubt, either, that the disparity between them arises to some extent, perhaps even to a considerable extent, from the kind of training they received. Broadly speaking, the first has had plenty of practice in bringing music to life with her own voice, whilst the second has concentrated on obtaining an elementary technique on an instrument which is singularly intractable except in the most skilful hands. Leaving aside the question of whether or not the piano is a suitable instrument for accompanying infant singing, there are weaknesses in the training of both these teachers. The first will certainly be handicapped on occasions by her inability to provide an accompaniment and might have benefited from some training in playing the recorder or guitar, or in the imaginative use of the auto-harp, chime-bars or the like. The second, on the other hand, has been set an exceptionally difficult task which has allowed her too little time to acquire a sense of style through re-creating music by more natural means. She too might have benefited from learning to play her accompaniments on a less exacting instrument.

This simple example illustrates the problem of 'balance' that in one way or another is found over the whole range of training music students. It also poses the question of 'standards'. Everybody concerned with training is anxious not only to maintain standards but to raise them. The only question is 'the standards of what?' It is easier to assess standards in the tangible than in the intangible aspects of music. It is easier, in piano playing, to assess accuracy of notes than flexibility of phrasing. It is easier to assess a student's ear by giving dictation tests than by listening to him holding his part in a madrigal. It is easier to assess a knowledge of harmony by written exercises than by practical work on an instrument. For this reason, and also so that the standard of the syllabus can be 'seen to be satisfactory', there is a natural tendency to prescribe various tangible things which it is thought that music teachers ought to be able to do. Some students may take these requirements in their stride and still have plenty of time to develop the even more important, intangible aspects of music. Others, however, may find them so difficult that they have little time left for developing an artistic sense of performance. In their case, taken all in all, the desire to raise standards by requiring certain specific skills may actually lead to the reverse effect.

There is one other aspect of teaching training that gives perennial cause for discussion and that is whether main, and even subsidiary, subjects should be studied purely for the student's personal development or whether they should include the pedagogics of the subject also. In music, fortunately, this is very largely an academic point. The best way of teaching music students (if so presumptive a term may, for convenience, be used) is so closely related to the best way of teaching children that the student can hardly fail to absorb plenty of professional expertise without any special effort. The best way embraces a wide variety of content and approach but, it is generally agreed, would include a great deal of creative and re-creative music making, tuition on an appropriate instrument, a realistic method of aural training which might include vocal and instrumental improvisation and a broad basis of general musical knowledge. Students who follow such a course and who are encouraged to take regular charge of their own group normally approach the problems of class teaching with far more confidence than those who have followed a more academic course entirely under the direction of their lecturers. Generally speaking they also have a more artistic approach to music.

Personal Musicianship

It is widely recognised that any artist, to keep in trim, must periodically engage in some activity beyond the scope of what he is normally required to do professionally. The orchestral player needs to do some solo work or chamber music, the organist must occasionally give a recital as well as play his church services, the lieder singer

sometimes appears on the operatic stage. The teacher-artist must do
the same, both to sharpen his musical perception and maintain and
increase his technical accomplishments. It does not much matter
what he decides to do, as long as it is something that appeals to him
primarily as a musician and is not directly concerned with schools.
His school work will certainly benefit indirectly. For example, if he
makes a thorough study of Schubert's *Winter Journey*, either as
singer or accompanist, it will given him an insight into 'school' songs
that will last him the rest of his life. On a different but also a desirable
level, membership of a serious folk group, either as guitarist or
singer, would accomplish much the same thing. Madrigal singing,
accompanying, chamber music playing, composition and (if well
done) conducting are all exacting and enthralling musical disciplines
that can hardly fail to quicken a musician's sensitivity. Choral
singing and orchestral playing, though demanding less individual
initiative, also provide valuable refreshment and experience.

Apart from activities such as these, many teachers seek to improve
their technique by taking lessons from time to time, as, indeed, do
many distinguished professional musicians. Whether the object of
such lessons is a periodical check-up or a long-term course of
instruction, it is rarely necessary, at the adult level, to take them every
week. It is important, however, to obtain the best advice available,
even if it involves considerable travel and, in the case of the long-
term objective, to follow it up by regular practice between lessons. It
is also important to avoid impatience for quick results. Musical
techniques take years rather than months to acquire but, if based
upon sound principles, they last for life. It is rarely too late to begin.
Whatever the result, the struggle is satisfying in itself and, in any case,
real understanding of music comes only to those who have made the
effort to find out through practical experience what it takes to be a
musician.

Interpretation

Nobody can learn how to interpret music from a book. Personal
guidance backed up by plenty of practical experience is the only way.
As it can be useful, however, to keep a few basic principles in mind,
and as the ability to interpret music lies at the root of success as a
music teacher, a few general observations are offered here.

The first thing to remember about interpretation is that music has a
logic of its own which, even in songs, is independent of words.
Musicians often speak of music 'making sense' or of having a 'satisfactory shape'. Beethoven, as may be seen from his sketchbooks, was
aiming for this sort of clarity when moulding this poignant phrase
from the slow movement of the first Razoumovsky Quartet; his

intentions are clearly revealed in the final version, which obviously has far more definition than the first.

Ex. 3

Ex. 4

These small points of timing, emphasis, tension and so on, emerging from a medium which is confined to sound spaced out in time, comprise the entire material with which the interpretative musician has to deal. It is up to him to weigh them carefully and see that the musical image comes out clear, not blurred or warped.

The second thing to keep in mind is that interpretation has to be worked out through the head and not the hands. Some people never stop to think, modestly excusing themselves on the grounds that they cannot hear music clearly in their head. It is probably true to say that nobody, except the very greatest of musicians, can hear music mentally with the same clarity as if listening to an actual performance but, though he may not hear everything, almost any musician has a better chance of perceiving the general shape of the music if he pauses periodically during his practising and thinks out mentally exactly what he is trying to do. A few minutes thought, in the long run, is also much quicker than trial and error on voice or instrument.

Tempo should always be considered first, as it is much the most important factor in interpretation. If the tempo is right other difficulties such as enunciation and intonation frequently solve themselves; indeed, if they persist, it is always advisable to reconsider the tempo before dealing with them separately. Unfortunately there is no golden rule and everyone must think things out himself. Generally speaking, there is a tendency to take fast music too slowly and slow music too fast. One must be realistic, however, and adapt to circumstance. For instance, the delightfully lazy tempo at which a bass might sing a negro spiritual could be too slow to support the phrasing of lighter voices. Confusion sometimes arises through misconception of the basic beat. Many songs (*Sweet Nightingale*, for example) although commonly written in 3/4 have a basic beat of one-in-a-bar. Similarly, many songs written in 4/4 should be sung in 2/2, a very different story. Perhaps the classic instance is *Nymphs and*

Shepherds, which appears in 4/4 in at least one well known school edition. The reason may be seen from the Purcell Society Edition, where it was originally written in 2/2, a time-signature which, on the very same page, the editor changed to 4/4 for the continuo part, with the addition of a cautionary *Allegro Moderato* of his own; others have followed this marking since, although at this slow speed the vocal runs are extremely difficult to sing. Another misconception is the meaning of the term *Largo* which, even in the late eighteenth century, was still regarded as a 'middle tempo'; *Where e'er you walk*, therefore, should not go nearly as slowly as it is sometimes taken (in the composer's manuscript it is marked *Largo e pianissimo per tutto*). It need hardly be added that, in traditional songs, the clue to the tempo lies in the words and the vocal line, not in the piano accompaniment.

An underlying flexibility of rhythm is implicit in all music, although it can rarely be indicated in the score. Rhythm can be metronomic, or it can lean forward on its tempo, or back on it. Some teachers give a verbal impression of these characteristics by referring to a steady tune, or a slippery tune, or a sticky tune. Metronomic rhythm, as distinct from relaxed dance rhythm such as the Viennese waltz, is comparatively rare, although Schubert uses it with powerful effect to portray horror, relentlessness and vacancy of mind, and it is occasionally found elsewhere. It is one thing, however, to maintain a rigid rhythm for some purpose of this kind and quite another to do so because one cannot think of anything else to do. Unless there is some good reason to the contrary, music always has a forward or a backward pull. *Blow away the morning dew*, for instance, leans forward on its tempo whereas *The raggle-taggle gypsies* leans back on it. Very often the implicit pull of the rhythm varies almost from bar to bar. Sometimes, contrariwise, it has a drag on the melody at the same time as a forward incline in the accompaniment, as in many American negro blues and even in such an apparently innocent song as Brahms's *Ladybird*, which, although appearing in some infant songbooks, has a nostalgia that is far from childlike.

In songs, fortunately, the words are usually a considerable help in moulding the phrasing, indeed in some songs it is only by 'relishing the words' that a convincing melodic line can be obtained. Handel's *Silent Worship* (as it is known in the English version), a difficult song to bring off effectively, is a case in point. Here it is necessary to make the most of the vowels coinciding with the beats, especially 'lady', where false accentuation frequently occurs. It is also necessary to make a point of articulating 'you not' evenly in order to avoid the common error of shortening the first note of a duplet and thus upsetting the smoothness of the phrase.

Ex. 5

Did you not hear my la - dy

Although the words are usually a help it is necessary to beware of inadequate translations which, as in a familiar edition of *The Trout*, may baffle singer, accompanist and listeners alike.

One or two points which apply perhaps more to instrumental than to vocal music may be mentioned in conclusion. It is not always realised that in the seventeenth and eighteenth centuries dotted notes were automatically double-dotted. For instance, the rhythm of the Air from Handel's *Water Music*, which can all too easily sound sluggish if played as written, is immediately given point if the quavers are double-dotted, or very nearly so.

Ex. 6

Another common problem is the dogged thump of the first beat in the bar. It is at its worst in and here, as in many other figures in compound time, it can be helpful to hinge the rhythm to the final quaver of the bar, in other words to skip rather than march to a 6/8 tune; in string music this would be helped by bowing

 . In all music, in fact, lightening unimportant first beats is one of the most necessary things the interpreter has to do.

Conducting

Almost any teacher of music is called upon at one time or another to take charge of a performance of some kind, that is to conduct. Conducting in this sense can range from giving a simple lead on an accompanying instrument, much as the continuo player did in the eighteenth century, to directing a large choral and orchestral work with a baton. Other things being equal, the conductor should select whatever method suits him best. In any case, his first job is to set the speed. This is not as easy as it seems and needs plenty of private practice if it is to be done with assurance and certainty. The conductor must have the tempo firmly in his mind before he starts and, to that end, should think hard of some characteristic phrase in the music (not necessarily from the beginning of the piece) which he has selected for that purpose beforehand. Once the beat is going strongly in his mind he can convey it to the singers or players by unobtrusive rhythmic movements of his head, lips or hands, and communication will be helped if he commands their attention with his eyes. Preliminary movements of this kind become less necessary with increased experience on both sides, but it is always essential to give one preparatory gesture to start the music off. This is what some inexperienced conductors find difficult, but it is really little more than the breath which singers take instinctively before they start to sing. If the conductor will think of it this way and actually take a breath in the tempo of the beat, he need only match it with a slight lift of the head, the shoulders or the arms, and follow it with a downward gesture on the following beat to show exactly where the performers should come in. This applies equally to entries coming on a sub-division of the beat, which children nearly always fit in correctly if the conductor does not fuss them with hurried subsidiary beats. New verses and restarts after a pause should obviously be treated in the same way as beginnings, the secret always being a clear preparatory beat. If in doubt, a mirror is always a helpful critic.

A rhythmic start in the right tempo is undoubtedly half the battle and many a verse or complete song requires little else. It is useful, however, to develop a clear 'beat' with which to keep the rhythm alive should it be required. The simpler it is the better. A baton is rarely needed except for orchestral conducting and, if none is used, there is no need to follow the conventional pattern of the different beats in the bar. A perfectly effective beat for most practical purposes can easily be developed from rhythmic tapping on the knee, which many people do quite naturally when listening to music sitting in a chair; one need only give the wrist a good upward spring and continue the same movement standing up, with the arm in much the same position relative to the body. The upward movement, it may be added, is a great psychological aid in maintaining lightness and pitch, and is thus far more important than the down, which if over-emphasised often has the reverse effect.

The conductor should give this kind of rhythmic stimulus whenever it seems to be required but it is rarely necessary to do so all the time. For the rest he should use his gestures to mould the phrasing, indicate dynamics, bring out points of emphasis and so on, and he should remember that even at a climax in the music a bold upward gesture has more life in it than a strenuous downward one. None of these gestures needs to be particularly large, in fact the extravagant conductor reaps much the same reward as the teacher who perpetually shouts, but it is obviously important that he should place himself where everyone can see him clearly from waist upwards. Although economy of movement is most desirable, unflagging concentration, focussed through eyes, lips and facial expression, is essential. It can have a powerful telepathic effect and if it falters the children will almost certainly falter too. Confidence, in fact, is the keynote of success and, though he may be nervous himself, the conductor should always make a point of putting his young performers at their ease. A smile all round is the simplest way. It is equally important to preserve freshness by avoiding the temptation to rehearse too much. Most music should be learnt as quickly as possible and then either rested or performed before staleness has set in.

This sort of instinctive conducting, arising naturally from the music itself, is quite sufficient for most purposes in schools, but some teachers may wish to go further and learn to use a baton. In doing so, they should realise that the baton is a precision tool and that it should be used as such. It is required, for instance, for the precise timing of a woodwind chord, or accompanying recitative or obtaining tidy pizzicato from the strings. Because it is a precision tool it demands absolute clarity of intention and is thus particularly valuable in training a conductor to think out clearly exactly what his intentions really are. Every movement, in fact, must have its purpose. If he will use the baton in this way it will increase both his effectiveness as a conductor and his musical understanding. If he uses it merely as a rigid extension of his arm for the instinctive type of conducting that has just been described, it will do no good at all.

Any teacher contemplating the use of the baton is advised to attend a course or take some lessons, as he would if learning a new musical instrument. It takes nearly as long to come to terms with a baton as it does with a bow. Properly used, the baton becomes a light and flexible extension of the arm manipulated mainly by the fingers, and daily practice, certainly for a year or two, is needed to make it second nature. Apart from advice from an experienced conductor or orchestral player, a mirror is as good a guide as any. Recitatives, concertos, Italian opera, indeed any music in which it is necessary to follow a soloist, provide the best material on which to learn, as realistic practice can be obtained from recorded or broadcast performances. Sooner or later the student may find that he has followed the soloist more faithfully than the conductor in the studio and he will then be ready to direct a live performance of the work himself. Whether or

not that opportunity ever comes he will still have learnt a great deal
that will help him to conduct at a more modest level.

Accompanying and Arranging

It has been suggested earlier in this chapter that the traditional form
of accompaniment on the piano is not always the most appropriate.
Some carols and folk songs could be accompanied more suitably with
no more than a tambourine. The accompanist, therefore, should be
prepared to adapt himself to circumstances and, even when sticking
to the piano, should be able to lay out his accompaniments in different ways. These aspects of his work are considered later. For the time
being it is enough to consider his function as an accompanist of
Lieder and other songs in which he is not called upon to vary the
actual notes.

Most songs begin with an introduction; if they do not, it is usually
easy enough to provide one by borrowing the last line or so of the
verse. The purpose of an introduction is to set the scene and provide a
springboard for the singer. The accompanist, therefore, must think
himself into the mood of the song before he starts and, having started
well, must not throw his advantage away by slackening tempo before
the singer's entry, as if anticipating hesitancy. Even quite young
children are perfectly capable of coming in rhythmically with a little
practice, but they can hardly be expected to do so with confidence on
a sagging rhythm. The same principle applies to piano interludes in
the middle of the song. Perhaps the classic instance is the accompanist's solo bar in Schubert's *To Music*. If there is any loss of tension
here, as there sometimes is, it is quite impossible for the singer or
singers to come in convincingly with the ecstatic following phrase.

Ex. 9

Hast thou my heart—

In this respect long notes in the voice part are barely different from
rests. It is still up to the accompanist to provide the rhythmic vitality
that is required and his musicianship will be remorselessly revealed
even in such a well known example as 'Comfort Ye' from *Messiah*.

Ex. 10

Com - - - fort ye

When accompanying children the accompanist must also take a lead in suggesting many points which an adult soloist would make without prompting. He can suggest lightness by staccato playing, a climax by leading the crescendo, a breathing point by a comma, a key word by an accent and so on. A skilled accompanist, in fact, can transform the phrasing of a song by split-second anticipation which only a very discerning listener would perceive as such. In the classroom, however, there is some risk of this prompting becoming exaggerated and crude. This is a danger that every teacher has to watch, partly for the sake of his own playing and partly because the children should be taught to rely upon themselves. The antidote is to seize every opportunity that offers itself of accompanying sensitively, sitting properly at the keyboard (not standing up) and exercising as much artistry and skill as if accompanying an adult soloist. This should be done whenever possible at every lesson.

The need for re-arranging accompaniments arises most of all with folk songs in primary schools and here, as well as the character of the music, the class teacher sometimes has to consider his limitations as an executant. It is far better to play a simplified accompaniment musically than attempt the written one mechanically. Unison or octave playing frequently gives adequate support and is capable of considerable variation through changes of register or spacing. This is particularly useful in songs of a repetitive kind where some variety is required. *Bobby Shaftoe* is a case in point. It is sufficient here to indicate the practicable extremes of left and right hand, which

Ex. 11

produce a very wide spacing such as Shostakovitch often uses to good effect in his chamber music.

Sometimes a light chord every bar, or every other bar, will provide all the support that is required. A few possible variants to the refrain of *Bobby Shaftoe* are given below.

Ex. 12

In music of a more flowing character a simple contrapuntal accompaniment is often more appropriate. Most good printed arrangements have a bass line which provides a satisfying counterpoint to the melody and which can be used without the rest of the harmony. *The little boy and the sheep*[25] is only one of an infinite variety of examples that might be given.

Ex. 13

Hymns are normally printed for four-part singing and, in both primary and secondary schools, are usually in need of re-arrangement; they are in fact, almost invariably adapted by church organists, if only by putting the bass line on the pedals. On the piano it is equally necessary to reinforce the bass and arrange the upper parts conveniently for the right hand. A four-part harmonisation of *St. Denio* and a piano version are indicated for comparison below, the latter with melody and bass in octaves, and the essential harmony note added; a simpler version is indicated for those with small hands.

Ex. 14

[25]From *Songs for Juniors.* Compiled by John Horton and published by Schofield and Sims.

A tromba stop can be simulated by close harmony in a lower register.

Ex. 15

A descant can also be provided by superimposing notes from the alto or tenor part.

Ex. 16

In carol festivities of various kinds, where children might be required to move about as they sing, it is useful to arrange accompaniments for simple portable instruments. *Patapan* obviously calls for side-drum and descant or sopranino recorder.

Ex. 17

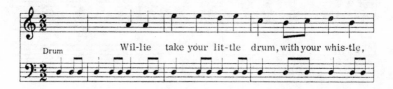

When the singers, or at any rate the players, do not move from place to place as they sing there are obviously infinite possibilities of arrangements using other simple percussion, melodic or chordal instruments. These add greatly to the children's interest and experience and, in any case, often provide a more appropriate accompaniment than the piano. Effective use can also be made of a small electronic organ. As with the piano this should be used mainly to supply an effect or a part (such as the bass) which is missing from the ensemble; it should rarely double the existing parts, particularly the melody at the same octave as another instrument (it may be noted that some printed accompaniments to recorder melodies offend in this respect, with the result that clarity is lost and the players are unable to listen critically to their own melodic line).

In all accompaniments variety is needed not only in arrangement and instrumentation but in key. When class melodic instruments are incorporated in ensemble accompaniments the choice of key is usually determined by the limits of the children's skill. The keys of C, G and D thus reappear with a frequency which tends, quite subconsciously, to induce monotony and fatigue. The teacher should therefore provide relief where possible by accompanying on the piano in some less familiar key. D flat and G flat, for example, are rarely used although they often involve no difficulty in transposition other than mental amendment of the key signature from sharps to flats; accompanists should remember that these and other less familiar keys provide a freshness of colour which children appreciate and respond to instinctively, even though they may be unaware of its cause.

Whether it is used to provide variety of key or to alter pitch to suit voices, transposition at the piano should not be regarded as an accomplishment confined only to highly competent musicians. Like everything else, it has degrees of skill. At its highest it may involve transposing difficult *Lieder* at sight. But there are many transpositions of simple song accompaniments which any moderate pianist can work out, or write out, before using them in class. And on the guitar the *capo* obviates the need even for this preparatory work.

Rehearsing

The most successful class teaching in music invariably smacks more of a rehearsal than a lesson. The heading of this section has been chosen to emphasise that point, although *Teaching* might actually be a more appropriate term. The success of the rehearsal method arises from the fact that not only is it more important for children to learn music than to learn about music but that, at all levels, they respond best to an approach that treats them more as performers than as pupils.

There is little difference in principle between rehearsing a symphony orchestra at the highest professional level and taking a music class in schools. Orchestral players always rise to a conductor who knows the works and his craft so well that he wastes neither time nor words. They appreciate someone who has done his preparation beforehand and is not learning on the orchestra, who can indicate his intentions by musical and not verbal means, who gives them a chance to play without constant stops, who does not rehearse things twice when once will do and who keeps them fresh for the performance. Children, no less human than professional musicians, respond much the same. They work well for a teacher who gets on with the job and does not talk too much. They respect someone who knows exactly how the music ought to go and can demonstrate quickly on voice or instrument, who gives them a good run at it and does not fuss them over every detail, who never allows them to get bored by aimless repetition.

It is essential that the teacher, like the professional conductor, should enter fully into the music he has chosen to rehearse. This means that it must appeal strongly to him personally and be suitable for adults as well as suitable for children. Self-interest, in this case, is a valuable safeguard of quality. It is also essential that the teacher, like the conductor, should keep himself musically alert by frequently teaching something fresh. Some instrumental pieces and songs undoubtedly wear better in rehearsal than others but even the greatest will not withstand unlimited repetition. And in this respect staleness is a greater danger to the teacher than it is to the children. An enterprising choice of good music that is within the children's powers is fundamental, therefore, if everyone's interest is to be fully engaged and maintained. A searching question to ask oneself at the end of any music lesson is 'Have both the children and I really enjoyed at least three good tunes during the past half-hour?'

Rehearsals (music lessons) can be organised in many different ways and variety adds greatly to their effectiveness. Generally speaking it is a good plan to aim at finishing off something that was begun last time, at breaking the back of something new and at running through something that has been learnt already. The more direct the approach, the more music it is possible to get through, but it is rarely a waste of time to discuss points of interpretation with the pupils as this always enlists their interest and encourages self-criticism. It might surprise some laymen to learn how critical even infants can become. The opportunity of an actual performance periodically, perhaps at assembly or some other domestic occasion of that kind, also adds point to the rehearsals, as much for individual forms as for the school choir or orchestra.

Most rehearsals in schools must also include some training in musicianship and general musical knowledge. It is nearly always advisable to relate this in some way to the music that is being rehearsed. Almost any piece of music that is worth doing provides ample opportunity for practice in music reading, for teaching some new technical term and for imparting a little information about its composer, form, instrumentation or something of that kind. Small pieces of information let fall casually in this way are often remembered when more systematic instruction has been forgotten and they also leave more time for other things. Balancing the teaching against the rehearsing is a problem every teacher must solve himself. However he does it, it is advisable to check up periodically by asking himself, 'How much good music that is new to them have I rehearsed with this group this term?'.

8

Administration

This chapter is intended principally for administrators and heads of schools who may find it convenient to have a synopsis of the main points about the organisation of music, apart from pedagogics. It is purposely brief. Further information can be obtained from previous chapters or from Chapter 9, *References*.

Primary Schools

The sort of provision outlined in Building Bulletin No. 23, *Primary School Plans: A Second Selection* (HMSO 1964) is basically sufficient. The development of instrumental playing should be kept in mind, and practical spaces which can be used for instrumental tuition, amongst other things, should be provided if possible. Storage for instruments is also important.

Middle Schools

Specific accommodation for music is desirable and, in fact, accommodation for music and drama is envisaged in all the examples of new middle schools given in Building Bulletin No. 35, *New Problems in School Design: Middle Schools* (HMSO 1966). This bulletin also contains examples of centres for music and drama among possible extensions which might be made in order to convert existing primary schools to middle schools.

Secondary Schools

Advice on planning, including school halls, is given in Building Bulletin No. 30: *Secondary School Design, Drama and Music* (HMSO 1966), which is also applicable to the replanning of existing premises. A particular problem arises in schools accommodated in

76

two or three separate buildings. If possible, it is best to concentrate the music accommodation in one building where some small rooms for instrumental work and a large rehearsal room can be contrived, in addition to two or three ordinary music rooms to accommodate classes of about 30 pupils. Advice is given in Building Bulletin No. 40, *New Problems in School Design: Comprehensive Schools from Existing Buildings* (HMSO 1968). At least one authority (Kent) has made successful use of prefabricated, movable music rooms.

Schools with a Music Bias

The following comprises the relevant sections of the approved schedule of accommodation of the proposed High School of Art and Music in Manchester, to which reference was made in Chapter 5. The provision for practising rooms should be noted in particular.

PART 1   1. Local Education Authority—MANCHESTER

           2. School—HIGH SCHOOL OF ART

           3. The following details relate to the complete school:

	Initial five year course	*Sixth Form*	*Total*
Number of Pupils:			
11+ entry	600	120	720
13+ entry	90	30	120
16+ entry		30	30
	690	180	870
Minimum teaching area	30,915 sq.ft.	8,910 sq.ft.	39,825 sq.ft.
Places for cost purposes	773	223	996
Plus 3 per cent for 95 per cent dining (to nearest five places)			1,026
Number of form units	23	6	29

PART 2   *Schedule of Accommodation*

Group	Teaching Space	No. of Spaces	Area of each space sq. ft.	Total Area of each Group sq. ft.	No. of teaching spaces	No. of form bases
A	Assembly Hall (Note 3a)	1	3,200		1	
	Small Hall (Note 3b)	1	1,200		1	
	Gymnasium	1	2,800		2	
					(enc. swimming pool on site)	
	Music Recital (Note 3b)	1	1,120		1	1 ⎫ Note
	Second Music Room					⎬ 3f
	(Note 3b)	1	800		1	1 ⎭
	Instrumental Practice Rooms Note 3b)	6	150 ⎫			
	Individual Practice Rooms (Note 3b)	35	60 ⎭		1	
				12,120		
B	Library (Note 3c)	1			—	
	Library Classroom	1	600		1	1 ⎫ Note
	Division Rooms (Note 3c)	6	250		—	3 ⎬ 3f
	Sixth Form Common Room	1	800		1	2 ⎭
				4,500		
C	*General Teaching Rooms*					
	Classrooms (Note 3d)	5	720		5	5
		10	540		10	10
				9,000		
D	*Practical Accommodation*					
	Science Laboratories	4	960		4	
	Housecraft	2	960		1	
	Dress Crafts	2	850		2	2 ⎰ Note
						⎱ 3f
	Wood/Metalwork	1	1,400		1	
	Textile Crafts (Note 3e)	1	850		1	
	Modelling and Pottery (Note 3e)	1	1,200		1	
	Drawing and Painting (Note 3e)	1	1,200		1	1 ⎫
	General Art/Craft (Note 3e)	2	840		2	2 ⎬ Note 3f
		1	850		1	1 ⎭
				14,640		
	Totals:	85		40,260	38	29

PART 4   NOTES

1. The schedule is based on an entry of pupils at 11+, 13+ and 16+ years of age as detailed in Part I above with probably a few more girls than boys.
2. The social organisation will be by forms.
3. (a) The assembly hall will also be used for physical education on occasion.
      It is proposed that a pipe organ should be provided in the assembly hall and that provision should be made for an orchestra pit (which could be by dividing off the requisite floor area by a removable rail arrangement).
   (b) The small hall should be available as a third music room and should be planned in close association with the other music rooms.
      Careful acoustic insulation from the kitchen (e.g. by interposing the chair store) will be required.
      The number of individual practical rooms is based on a 1-form entry seven year course and making a minimum allowance for one period of practice per pupil per day. Practice rooms could be made available out of school hours to students whose hostels will adjoin the school site.
      Musical practice rooms should be soundproof and careful attention should be paid to acoustics in the performing areas.
   (c) The division rooms are to be planned in pairs with retractable partitions; some at least should adjoin the library, library-classroom and VIth form common room.
      The library should have two or three associated listening booths for hearing records and additional storage space for a records library.
   (d) One of the 720 square feet classrooms is to be planned in association with the laboratories.
   (e) The Inspector and Organiser for Art and the Headmaster are to be consulted at an early stage in planning about the disposition of these rooms. Very generous storage accommodation is required for the art and craft rooms.
   (f) 330 lockers to be provided in a suitable part of the circulation areas outside these rooms.
   (g) Instrument storage needs careful consideration. It might be necessary to plan for up to 150 instruments which pupils will want to deposit immediately on arrival at school. It is suggested that storage might be provided in association with the cloakroom areas.

Music Centres

These can provide specialised instruction for musically talented children of all ages, supplement the work in schools and help to bridge the gap between school and adult music making. A report published in 1966 by the Standing Conference for Amateur Music, *Music Centres and the Training of Specially Talented Children*, gives information about some existing centres and offers suggestions for establishing new ones. For practical purposes a music centre may be taken to include almost any centralised arrangement for tuition, study or performance. Also see Chapter 5, page 49.

EQUIPMENT

Musical instruments are basic equipment in the same sense as climbing apparatus in the primary school or lathes and cookers in the secondary school. If a reasonable stock is not provided at the outset, schools have little hope of obtaining an adequate supply from annual allowances or by paying half the cost themselves (a requirement that can usually be met, however, once adequate basic provision has been made).

As there is a considerable overlap in the needs of primary and secondary schools, some infant equipment being equally suitable at the secondary stage, it is impossible to specify precise requirements at the different levels. The following suggestions simply provide a general guide. British Standards have been issued for most of the items quoted and administrators are urged to consult the relevant publications (see Chapter 9) for advice on purchase, installation and maintenance. It is advisable to instal humidifiers in centrally heated rooms in which instruments are regularly kept, unless an air conditioning plant already makes provision for humidity control.

Pianos and Harpsichords

It is essential to have a piano with a sufficient length of string to support massed singing in the school hall. In secondary schools this usually implies a grand of 6 foot length or more. Sizeable uprights, having a longer length of string than baby grands, are usually adequate for primary school halls. Further instruments, which can be smaller, are needed in all rooms where class music lessons are regularly given, although in some cases a small electronic organ may be used instead. Adjustable piano stools are needed for every piano. It is suggested that piano tuning and maintenance is carried out on the lines recommended by B.S.I.

A portable harpsichord, which could be lent out as required, adds considerably to the musical work of an area. It might normally be kept in a music centre or music department of a large school.

Guitars and Harps

The guitar is being used increasingly in primary schools as an accompanying instrument and the Celtic harp is occasionally found. Either or both might be supplied if likely to be used effectively by individual teachers. The guitar is also used for class instruction, and may be supplied in much the same way as orchestral or brass band instruments.

Electronic Equipment

Small portable electronic organs are now available at a cost comparable with that of a new upright piano and are of value as a second keyboard instrument.

Every school needs a good record player with an extension speaker, a stock of records and a tape recorder; in primary schools these are sometimes kept on a trolley; in secondary schools each room used for full-time music teaching should be equipped with both these items, which are essential for day to day work. Sound of adequate quality will be ensured if schools insist on the British Standard specification for such equipment. On record players a groove locator free from creep and backlash, and accurate within one or two microgrooves, is considered essential.

All schools should have sound radio and television; large music departments need a separate V.H.F. tuner.

Power points should be conveniently placed if the best use is to be made of electronic equipment.

Instruments for Class Use

A wide variety of easy instruments are now available which can be used, at all stages, for class instruction and class participation in simple orchestrations of various kinds. Percussion instruments usually come first and they should include not only those of the purely rhythmic kind (triangles, tambourines, cymbals, drums and the like) but several melodic percussion instruments as well (for example, chime bars, glockenspiels and xylophones). Simple stringed instruments such as the nordic lyre, zither and bowed psaltery, which can be made in schools (see Chapter 9, 1, (j)) are being increasingly used, and the guitar, although it also lends itself to far more advanced playing, is often included to provide a simple chordal accompaniment. Instruments such as the melodica and the harmonica can also be justified if used artistically. In all cases it should only be necessary to obtain two or three of each instrument, the objective being the artistic contribution of several instruments rather than the massed playing of any one, or any one group, of them.

Recorders

These are used both as an aid in teaching music to complete classes and for more advanced ensemble playing in small groups. In either case it is important that all the instruments used together should be of the same make. For classwork, plastic descant recorders are adequate. For ensemble playing, good wooden instruments are preferable and they should include at least two trebles and a tenor. A bass recorder may be added to complete the consort. Arrangements for safe storage are important.

Brass Band Instruments

Brass playing is becoming increasingly common in schools. A start can be made with the cornet, leading to simple ensemble playing comprising, perhaps, two B flat cornets, one E flat horn and one B flat euphonium.

In secondary schools, if possible, it is best to aim for the immediate formation of a complete band, for which the minimum requirements would be:

5 B flat cornets
3 E flat horns
2 B flat baritones
1 B flat euphonium
1 E flat bass

All instruments should be of standard (low) pitch, i.e. A=440.

Stringed Instruments

Most children might be expected to buy their instruments after about a year and some schools and authorities assist them in this by arranging for hire purchase. A basic stock of violins is needed, however, sufficient in number for all the beginners at any one time. In primary schools this should include some three-quarter or even half size violins. All instruments should be fitted and maintained in accordance with B.S.I. recommendations.

A stock of the larger instruments will be needed for developing string teaching in secondary schools, two violas, two cellos, and a double bass being the smallest practicable unit. The viola and 'cello may be started in the junior school, using small instruments or, in the case of the viola, a large violin fitted and tuned a fifth lower than normal.

Orchestral Wind Instruments

These are expensive and, although children are often willing to purchase their own in course of time, it is unreasonable to expect them to do so at the outset. The school should enable them to make a start. The flute and the clarinet can be started at the top of the primary school but the oboe and the bassoon are best left to the secondary stage, as is orchestral brass (as distinct from brass band instruments). Initially the orchestral brass might comprise two trumpets and two trombones, or two trumpets, French horn and trombone, which constitute a satisfactory ensemble in themselves.

Miscellaneous Equipment

Metal music stands will be needed for all types of instrumental work, except piano teaching. One stand for every two players would be reasonable initial provision. A set of light desk music rests will also be required for recorder playing in class.

At least one tuning fork (A=440) should be available, and also a clockwork metronome.

Furniture and Fittings

Furniture for a music classroom should be capable of easy rearrangement. Stackable chairs with firm seats and light stackable tables are recommended. Chair and table legs should be fitted with rubber tips. If the room has to do duty as a form base, lockers should be provided (preferably in the corridor outside) to obviate the need for locker-type desks.

Every teacher concerned with the subject in a junior or secondary school, whether as a specialist or as a general form teacher, should have at his disposal at least one chalk-board clearly painted with five-line staves. Blank chalk-board surfaces also are essential.

Display boarding is invaluable in the music room, and may also be found useful for music purposes in corridors or other circulation space.

Printed Music

Individual copies of hymn books are desirable, and if it is not possible to provide all junior or secondary pupils with the melody edition of the hymn book, one form set at least should be available for teaching purposes. In secondary schools some copies of the full harmony edition will be needed for older pupils and staff. Apart perhaps from the teaching set, hymn books should not be chargeable to the music department's annual allowance.

The allowance made for printed material in junior and secondary schools should cover song books and sheet music in sufficient variety to suit the different ages, aptitudes and interests of all the pupils in the school. On no account should 'words only' editions of song books be accepted. Attention should be drawn to Copyright (see Chapter 9).

Half-form sets of miniature scores are needed for secondary schools. Much of the success of instrumental training depends upon the early provision, not only of suitable individual and class material, but also of graded ensemble music. Allowances should also be made for percussion and recorder music.

Books, Pictures and Printed Music

Text-books of harmony and musical history will be needed for specialists preparing for external examinations, but a much wider selection of background material should be provided in the school library. The library should also contain printed music and records for general borrowing.

Apart from normal illustrative material, a few good pictures associated with music should be hung in rooms used for music or at appropriate points about the school. These might include pictures produced by the children themselves, for which suitable frames and display facilities should be provided.

Equipment for Special Schools

Equipment for music is at least as important in special schools as in normal schools. Most of the equipment listed above is suitable, but in some cases instruments have to be specially adapted. Suggestions of instruments and of adaptations to instruments suitable for different types of disability are obtainable from Disabled Living Activities Group, 39, Victoria Street, London, S.W.1.

STAFFING

Most music teaching in primary schools is done by class teachers, partly to enable them to bring music informally into the work as a whole and partly to avoid too much interchange of staff.

On musical grounds there is much to be said for some specialisation, however, if there is a capable musician on the staff; in any case, such a teacher should be encouraged to help class teachers who are less experienced, organise activities out of class and co-ordinate the work of visiting instrumental teachers. Although it is not ideal, some schools have made up for the lack of a capable musician on the full-time staff by appointing a part-time music teacher. Some authorities have arranged for specialist music teachers to be shared between two or three primary schools and occasionally the music specialist in a secondary school does a little teaching in a neighbouring primary school. In extreme cases the employment of a visiting accompanist might be justified.

Large secondary schools need a head of department enjoying much the same prestige as the director of music has traditionally held in public schools and having as much time for administration as, say, a teacher-librarian. In order to attract suitable applicants it is necessary to offer not only adequate salary but adequate scope for the development of voluntary activities, if necessary by pooling the work of two or three departments or schools. Ideally the head of music should be something of an impresario, as well as a good musician, teacher and organiser, and he should be encouraged to keep in touch with adult music making in the neighbourhood. Supporting staff should have complementary abilities and any large music department should include one full-time teacher with special experience of instrumental work. Visiting instrumental teachers or instructors may also be required.

Music centres need a principal with a large measure of independence, graded perhaps as a head of department on the further education scale. Some other staff working full-time in the centre may also be required as well as others who, though employed full-time by the authority, spend some of their time in schools.

Instrumental teachers are sometimes employed independently by schools but, especially in the case of the less common instruments, individual schools are often unable to offer sufficient work to make it worth a teacher's while. It is usually best for such teachers[26] to be employed on a peripatetic, and preferably a full-time, basis by the authority and paid an appropriate travelling allowance (as they frequently have to carry instruments and music, a car allowance is often justified, even in urban areas). To attract good players and maintain their freshness as teachers it is advisable to offer reasonable variety in the work; for example, some authorities employ their peripatetic instrumental staff for three days teaching in schools, one day coaching in a music centre and one day rehearsing and performing to children in a small ensemble. The appointment of an expert recorder player should not be overlooked. A note on the training of instrumental teachers in general is included below in the section on Local Authority Organisation. Heads of schools should regard visiting teachers as members of their staff and should ensure that at least one full-time teacher takes a personal interest in the instrumental teaching and is available to help the visiting staff as required.

Instrument maintenance and repair (including piano tuning) might well justify the employment of one or more suitable technicians.

SCHOOL ORGANISATION

In primary schools the flexible time-table and the relatively small number of children on the roll make the organisation of music comparatively easy.

It helps to have a spare teaching space but, to judge from what is often accomplished without this advantage, it is not essential. An instrumental trolley and another trolley for record player and tape recorder are very useful when equipment has to be moved from room to room. For some purposes a piano is not essential, but a small electronic organ which can be carried by a couple of children is becoming a useful adjunct. Taping broadcasts for schools enables them to be reproduced when most convenient (for legal conditions see Chapter 9). The value of instrumental tuition by visiting teachers is greatly enhanced if some supervised practice can be arranged. The musical opportunities offered by daily worship should be seized, and also opportunities for combining music, art and dance. The value of public performances, especially by very young children, should be judged on educational grounds and not on their effectiveness as a display for parents.

Secondary schools present more problems, partly because the time-table is often less flexible. Beyond a certain point it is impossible to

---

[26]Where qualified teachers are not available instructors may be employed in accordance with the conditions laid down in Circular 15/68, para. 23.

develop instrumental work without encroaching on school hours, i.e. some pupils must miss other work for their instrumental lessons, as they commonly do in primary, public and direct grant schools. The disadvantages of this arrangement can be minimised in a variety of ways; pupils who can least afford to miss other work are taught out of school hours; some instrumental pupils miss class music lessons; pupils have their instrumental lessons on a roster basis so that they do not miss the same class regularly; in a six or seven day time-table the instrumental lessons remain at the same time every week; conversely a six-day instrumental time-table rotates on a five day school time-table; half-hour instrumental lessons are superimposed on forty-minute class periods so that pupils can attend for a few minutes, e.g. to collect or hand in work.

Wide dispersal over two or more buildings is another problem, as it is best for all the musical work to be done in a properly equipped music wing in one building, an arrangement that is not easy to achieve without time-wasting movement during school hours. Advanced work at the 16–18 level can be time-tabled in three or four period blocks, which should avoid this difficulty, indeed some schools even allow half or whole day 'release' for pupils to attend a music centre for such work. Double periods are appropriate for the optional course at the 14–16 level, which should at any rate minimise the difficulty. The real problem arises with the basic course at the 11–14 level. The only answer here (for those forms which are not based in the same building as the music wing) is to arrange a combination of work which will keep them in that building for a complete day or half-day, e.g. a first year form might spend half-a-day there for daily worship, two periods art and craft, one period music and one period religious instruction. This is an actual example which worked successfully, indeed the headmaster said that, far from being a makeshift arrangement, the pupils benefited from the change of environment. The distribution of specialist rooms over the different buildings should therefore be thought out with this consideration in mind.

The third major problem is finding the time for voluntary musical activities. The benefits that such activities can bring both to the individual and to the school are widely recognised and the only matter for argument is how to fit them in. Sometimes they take place before school, e.g. to rehearse a choral introit or instrumental voluntary for daily worship. Where there is a reasonably concentrated catchment area a good deal can be done after school; in that case it is advisable to arrange that major activities such as the choir or orchestra have a recognised rehearsal time which is respected by other major school activities. Organisation is more difficult in schools with a wide catchment area, although the voluntary activities are no less important. Some schools finish early in order to provide time before the special buses depart. Others extend or stagger the mid-day break. Others, again, cater for voluntary activities within the traditional 9–4 timetable, whilst a few are experimenting with lengthening the school day. It may be added, in this connection, that in some American high schools a daily music rehearsal is time-tabled from 4 till 5 and that, in this country, most independent boarding schools which accept day boys do so on the condition that they spend virtually their whole time at the school apart from bed and breakfast, so that they can play a full part in the corporate life of the school.

LOCAL AUTHORITY ORGANISATION

The Music Adviser

In 1967, all but 35 of the 145 local education authorities in England employed a music adviser, including 17 authorities with a school population of less than 15,000; several authorities employed more than one adviser, in some cases four or five. As well as advising on such matters as staffing, accommodation, equipment and major awards the music adviser may also organise courses for teachers, instrumental tuition, concerts for schools and regional choirs, orchestras and festivals. His primary concern, however, will be work in schools, helping probationary teachers, passing on new ideas and so on and, although he may sometimes take over the direction of centralised musical events himself, he will doubtless also find opportunities of letting promising young music teachers try their hand and of bringing in distinguished musicians from outside.

Advisory Bodies

It is useful for the music adviser and the local authority to have some body to which they can turn, both to seek opinion and to obtain help in disseminating ideas. A branch of the Schools' Music Association or a County (or Borough) Music Committee can be helpful in these respects, as well as giving teachers and others a feeling that they have a worthwhile place in the district's musical activities.

It is desirable that such bodies should have a reasonable turn-over of membership and that young teachers should have a voice.

In Service Training

Experienced serving teachers applying for one-term and one-year courses are normally given leave of absence if accepted. This facility might be extended in exceptional circumstances to potentially good instrumental teachers who possess adequate practical experience but also need a course of training to obtain qualified teacher status, in which case the authority would take them nominally on its staff and immediately second them for an appropriate course. A very useful course for the general teacher is one which helps him to acquire some specific musical skill, say a weekly class extending over a year or more in instrumental playing or keyboard harmony or in preparation for a diploma in school music; in some cases authorities release teachers for such a course in school hours. A music-making weekend or holiday course, which need not necessarily be confined to teachers, can do much to stimulate musicianship and may well justify the payment of the same allowances that are applicable to courses of a purely pedagogic kind.

Almost any occasion for music teachers to discuss their work together is worth arranging, the many meetings throughout the country to formulate syllabuses for CSE having been particularly useful in this respect. Lectures on some aspect of teaching method also have their place, especially if backed up by practical work. One of the simplest and most effective ways of interchanging ideas is for teachers to visit other schools. In arranging courses of any kind liaison with neighbouring authorities, the area training organisation and local advisory bodies is desirable.

Instrumental Work

Most of the points concerning the organisation of instrumental tuition have already been covered earlier in this chapter under accommodation, music centres, equipment and staffing. It need only be repeated here that, to reach its potential, instrumental tuition should be organised on an area basis and not left entirely to individual schools.

The same might be said of some of the larger scale products of this tuition, namely bands and orchestras. Schools should undoubtedly be encouraged to develop smaller instrumental ensembles and orchestras of their own. Area organisation is required for two reasons; first, to cover the complete range of instruments needed, say, for a symphony, which few schools could supply without outside help; secondly, to offer opportunities for playing to a higher standard than individual schools might provide. These two claims of quantity and quality sometimes conflict but, if both are kept in mind, they can usually be balanced satisfactorily. Schools on the same campus sometimes run a joint orchestra. In compact urban areas, area orchestras can be organised with a rehearsal at some central point, usually on a regular evening during the week. In rural areas it is usual to hold rehearsals on a Saturday about once a month and to rehearse for the best part of the day; help with travelling is often given. Week-end or more extended holiday courses form a valuable follow-up and usually meet with an excellent response from the young players concerned. Whatever the arrangement may be, it is advisable to provide for some sectional work (and for the opportunity of playing chamber music) for which suitable accommodation and staff will be required. Although area orchestras benefit from having a permanent musical director (often the music adviser), a change of conductor is desirable from time to time; the better the orchestra the more necessary it will be to engage a professional conductor periodically.

Other Area Activities

These notes on orchestras also apply, in the main, to choirs. Area choral groups are useful if they provide opportunities beyond those available in individual schools, for example the performance of an opera or a major choral and orchestral work or madrigal singing of exceptional range and quality. At its simplest this might comprise no more than combining the resources of a neighbouring boys' and girls' school but obviously there are almost unlimited opportunities, including the production of opera. There is little value, however, in combining resources if nothing is added to the range of opportunity available in individual schools, indeed there is some danger that the range of opportunity might be actually limited thereby. This applies in particular to music festivals in which the massed singing of unison songs is the principal feature. Although these are often festive occasions and they may have some value as such, it should be recognised that musically there is nothing intrinsically better in the singing of 300 children than of 30 (particularly as some of the songs in most festival programmes were originally intended for solo singing) and, moreover, that some of the schools taking part may be diverted from more enterprising work of their own in consequence of the need to prepare for the festival. Festivals of this kind have sometimes outlived their usefulness as a means of introducing new songs into the schools and can only be justified on educational grounds nowadays if they provide some new and stimulating musical experience, which might include the services of a first-rate professional accompanist. However well it is run, it is not always desirable to hold this sort of festival every year.

These reservations do not apply to the 'audition session' of the traditional festival, which has much to be said for it. The essential features are that schools should present a normal sample of their work, not necessarily the best, that it should be commented on confidentially by a musician thoroughly conversant with music in schools (perhaps the music adviser or one of his colleagues from another authority) and that the auditions should be followed by a short conference, perhaps over tea, at which points of a general nature arising during the day might be discussed.

Concerts for Schools

Attendance at public concerts, opera and ballet is often organised by individual schools in areas where these facilities are available, but it can sometimes be helpful for the authority to make some central arrangements for ticket concessions and travel. Concerts specifically for schools are mostly arranged by the authority, often in consultation with the local advisory body. Opinion differs as to the respective merits of the recital by a soloist or small ensemble in the school itself and of attendance by pupils at a large scale performance at some central theatre or concert hall. On the whole most teachers favour the more personal appeal of the former, whilst regarding the latter as a desirable follow-up. Whatever is decided certain general points should be kept in mind. First, the standard of performance should be impeccable and should demand as much from the players as a public concert for adults; concerts given in schools by inadequately rehearsed groups of players assembled purely for the occasion are not good enough. Secondly, the programme should be short and suitable; none of the items should be too long and the programme should be well contrasted as a whole; some concert-givers need advice on programmes for schools. Thirdly, the authority is paying for musical expertise and not for instruction which could be given equally well, and perhaps better, in the classroom before-hand; the proportion of performance to explanation should therefore be as high as possible; it is a mistake to concentrate only on music that has to be explained (programme music, for example); if suitable music is chosen it can largely speak for itself.

9

References

This short list of references is intended merely to provide a convenient starting point for lines of inquiry. It makes no pretence to be exhaustive.

Organisations

Department of Education and Science,
   Curzon Street,
   London, W.1.
   Telephone: 01–493 7070

The Arts Council of Great Britain,
   4 St. James's Square,
   London, S.W.1.
   Telephone: 01–930 9737

The Standing Conference for Amateur Music,
   26 Bedford Square,
   London, W.C.1.
   Telephone: 01–636 4066

The Rural Music Schools Association,
   Little Benslow Hills,
   Hitchin, Herts.
   Telephone: Hitchin (Herts) 3446

Schools Music Association,
   4 Newman Road,
   Bromley, Kent.

The Choir Schools Association,
   Cathedral Choir School,
   Ripon, Yorks.

Incorporated Society of Musicians,
   48 Gloucester Place,
   London, W.1.
   Telephone: 01–935 9791

The International Society for Music Education,
Manderschieder Strasse 35,
5000 Cologne Klettenberg,
Germany.

The English Folk Dance and Song Society,
Cecil Sharp House,
2 Regent's Park Road,
London, N.W.1.
Telephone: 01–485 2206

The Performing Right Society Ltd.,
29–33 Berners Street,
London, W.1.
Telephone: 01–580 5544

British Federation of Music Festivals,
106 Gloucester Place,
London, W.1.
Telephone: 01–935 6371

The National Federation of Music Societies,
29 Exhibition Road,
London, S.W.7.
Telephone: 01–584 5797

The National Operatic and Dramatic Association,
1 Crestfield Street,
London, W.C.1.
Telephone: 01–636 5655

The Composers' Guild of Great Britain,
10 Stratford Place,
London, W.1.
Telephone: 01–499 8567

The Royal School of Church Music,
Addington Palace,
Croydon, Surrey.
Telephone: 01–654 7676

The Music Advisers' National Association,
166 Loughborough Road,
West Bridgford,
Nottingham.

Association of Teachers In Colleges and Departments of Education,
151 Gower Street,
London, W.C.1.
Telephone: 01–387 1437

The Music Teachers' Association,
106 Gloucester Place,
London, W.1.
Telephone: 01–935 6371

The Music Masters' Association,
48 Gloucester Place,
London, W.1.
Telephone: 01–935 9791

The National Youth Orchestra of Great Britain,
11 Garrick Street,
London, W.C.2.
Telephone: 01–240 2619

The National Youth Orchestra of Wales,
Welsh Joint Education Committee,
30 Cathedral Road,
Cardiff.

The British Schools Orchestra,
Schools Music Association.
4 Newman Road,
Bromley, Kent.

The British Youth Symphony Orchestra,
Schools Music Association,
4 Newman Road,
Bromley, Kent.

The National Youth Brass Band of Great Britain,
67 Yarningdale Road,
King's Heath.
Birmingham, 14.

National Schools Brass Band Association,
2 Gray's Close,
Barton-Le-Clay,
Bedford.

The Society of Recorder Players,
26 Delamere Road,
London, W.5.

The Pipers' Guild,
4 Oakway,
Raynes Park,
London, S.W.20.

Musical Education of the Under Twelves,
43 Sutton Park Road,
Seaford,
Sussex.

The Disabled Living Activities Group
(Central Council for the Disabled),
39 Victoria Street,
London, S.W.1.
Telephone: 01-222 7487

The Society for Music Therapy and Remedial Music,
6 Westbourne Park Road,
London, W.2.

Council for Music in Hospitals,
7 Upper Duke's Drive,
Eastbourne, Sussex.
Telephone: Eastbourne 1918

Royal National Institute for the Blind,
224 Great Portland Street,
London, W.1.
Telephone: 01-387 5251

B.B.C. Music Division,
Yalding House,
Great Portland Street,
London, W.1.
Telephone: 01-580 4468

Central Gramophone Library,
(British Institute of Recorded Sound, Ltd.),
29 Exhibition Road,
London, S.W.7.
Telephone: 01-589 6603

Central Music Library,
Buckingham Palace Road,
London, S.W.1.
Telephone: 01-730 0446

The British Institute of Recorded Sound,
29 Exhibition Road,
London, S.W.7.
Telephone: 01-589 6603

The Galpin Society,
7 Pickwick Road,
Dulwich Village,
London, S.E.21.

The Educational Group of the Association of Musical Instrument Industries,
25 Oxford Street,
London, W.1.
Telephone: 01-437 9586

Publications

(a) Department of Education and Science

Qualifications for recognition as qualified teacher.
See Circular 15/68,
Administrative Memorandum 14/61

Programme of one year Courses and one term Courses for Qualified Teachers, published annually.

Programme of Short Courses, published annually.

A Compendium of Teacher Training Courses in England and Wales.

Building Bulletin No. 30:—*Secondary School Design: Drama and Music* (HMSO).

(b) Other publications by HMSO.

The Schools Council Examinations Bulletin No. 10 '*The Certificate of Secondary Education: Experimental Examinations in Music*'.

Central Youth Employment Executive, Ministry of Labour, 'Choice of Careers, booklet No. 101. Music'.

Government bookshops

Belfast 1:	80 Chichester Street
Birmingham 5:	35 Smallbrook, Ringway
Bristol 1:	50 Fairfax Street
Cardiff:	109 St. Mary Street
Edinburgh 2:	13a Castle Street
London:	P.O. Box 569, London S.E.1.
Manchester 2:	Brazennose Street

(c) '*Making Musicians*'

A report to the Calouste Gulbenkian Foundation (1965), 98 Portland Place, London, W.1.

(d) '*Music Centres and the Training of Specially Talented Children*'
'*Music and the Newsom Report*'
'*The Scope of Instrumental Music in Schools*'
'*The Training of Music Teachers*'
'*Specimen Planning Notes on Musical Requirements in School Buildings*'
'*Specimen Planning Notes on Musical Requirements in Further Education Colleges*'
'*A List of Charitable Trusts*'
'*Contemporary Choral Music for Use in Schools*'
'*Contemporary Orchestral Music for Use in Schools*'

All published for the Standing Conference for Amateur Music by The National Council of Social Service,
26 Bedford Square,
London, W.C.1.

(e) A pamphlet on the Early Stages of String Class Teaching by The Rural Music Schools Association.

(f) '*Music Teaching for the Enthusiast*' by Derrick Herdman,
Incorporated Association of Preparatory Schools Pamphlet No. 26,
Warren & Son Ltd.
Staple Garden,
Winchester, Hants.

(g) '*Outline of Musical Education*'
(Curwen No. 8351). A pamphlet published by The Incorporated Society of Musicians.

(h) '*A Guide to the Purchase and Care of Woodwind and Brass Instruments*'
The Schools Music Association.

(i) British Standards Institution,
British Standards House,
2 Park Street,
London, W.1.

are preparing, at the request of the Schools Music Association, a series of specifications and purchasing recommendations for musical equipment. Among the first to be published are:

B.S. 3499 Part 1	*Percussion instruments*
2A	*Recorders*
2B	*Clarinets*
3A	*Trumpet in B flat*
4A	*Pianofortes*
5	*Recommendations to purchasers of stringed instruments*
6	*Methods of tests for musical instruments*
7A	*Music stands*
7B	*Percussion instrument trolleys*
8A	*Record players, V.H.F. tuners, amplifiers and loudspeakers*
9A	*Recommendations to purchasers of electric guitars*
9B	*Amplifiers suitable for use with musical instruments*
P.D. 5273	*'How to look after a piano'*
P.D. 5286	*'Care and maintenance of stringed instruments'*

Others will include:

electronic organs, cornets, trombones, flutes, oboes.

The B.S.I. Certification Marking scheme (the kite mark) is associated with many of these specifications.

(j) *'Musical Instruments made to be Played'*
  R. Roberts. Dryad Press.

(k) Some Periodicals

  'Composer' (Composers' Guild of Great Britain, 10 Stratford Place, W.1.) Quarterly.

  'The Gramophone' (General Gramophone Publications Ltd., 379 Kenton Road, Kenton, Middlesex) Monthly.

  'Hi-Fi News' (Link House, Dingwall Avenue, Croydon, Surrey) A monthly journal of information about audio equipment.

  'Making Music' (Rural Music Schools Association, Little Benslow Hills, Hitchin, Herts.) Quarterly.

  'Music' (Pergamon Press Ltd., 4 Fitzroy Square, London W.1.) A quarterly journal of the Schools Music Association.

  'Music and Musicians' (Hansom Books Ltd., 16 Buckingham Palace Road, London, S.W.1.) Monthly articles about composers and performers.

'*Music in Education*' (Novello & Co. Ltd., 27 Soho Square, London, W.1.) A bi-monthly dealing specifically with music in schools.

'*Music and Letters*' (O.U.P., 44 Conduit Street, London, W.1.) Quarterly journal devoted to musicology.

'*The Music Review*' (Heffer & Sons Ltd., Cambridge) Quarterly journal devoted to musicology.

'*The Music Teacher*' (Montague House, Russell Square, London, W.C.1.) Monthly

'*Musical Opinion*' (26 Hatton Garden, London, E.C.1.) Monthly.

'*The Musical Times*' (Novello & Co. Ltd., 27 Soho Square, London, W.1.) England's oldest musical journal, a monthly addressed particularly to organists and choirmasters.

'*Opera*' (Rolls House Publishing Co. Ltd., Breams Buildings, London, E.C.4.) Monthly articles on all aspects of opera.

'*Records and Recordings*' (Hansom Books Ltd., 16 Buckingham Palace Road, London, S.W.1.) Monthly.

'*The Recorder and Music Magazine*' (Schott & Co. Ltd., 48 Great Marlborough Street, London, W.1.) A quarterly devoted to the recorder.

'*The Strad*' (Horace Marshall & Son Ltd., 8 St. John's Lane, London, E.C.1.) A monthly for amateur and professional string players.

'*Tempo*' (Boosey & Hawkes Ltd., 295 Regent Street, London, W.1.) Quarterly reviews of contemporary music.

Visual and Audio Aids

(a) Information about films and filmstrips can be obtained from:

(i) The Educational Foundation for Visual Aids,
     33 Queen Anne Street,
     London, W.1.
     Telephone: 01–636 5742
     or
   The Foundation Film Library,
     Brooklands House,
     Weybridge,
     Surrey.
     Telephone: Weybridge 47478
   who publish a list giving full details.

   New additions to the library are published in E.F.V.A's monthly magazine 'Visual Education'.

(ii) The Central Film Library,
Government Building,
Bromyard Avenue,
London, W.3.
Telephone: 01–743 5555

(iii) UNESCO,
Place de Fontenoy.
Paris-7ᵉ,
who publish an international catalogue called '*Films for music education and opera films*', giving the addresses of all distributors.

(b) Details of gramophone records currently available for purchase in this country are given in:

'*The Gramophone Classical Record Catalogue*'

'*The Gramophone LP Popular Record Catalogue*'—quarterly. (Both are issued quarterly by General Gramophone Publications Ltd., 379 Kenton Road, Kenton, Middlesex.)

'*Penguin Guide to Bargain Classics*' (Penguin Books Ltd.)

'*A Guide to the Bargain Classics*' (Long Playing Record Library Ltd., Squires Gate, Blackpool).

(c) Gramophone records can be borrowed, on certain conditions, from:

The Central Gramophone Library,
29 Exhibition Road,
London, S.W.7.
Telephone: 01–589 6603

Some municipal libraries. A list of these is available from:
The Library Association,
7 Ridgmount Street,
London, W.C.1.
Telephone: 01–636 7543

Further Musical Education

Some universities provide degree courses in music which place emphasis on the scholarly rather than on the practical side, and some include music as a subject in a general arts degree course.

London University works with the Royal Academy of Music, Trinity College and the Royal College of Music, and the Manchester University with the Royal Manchester College of Music, to provide a joint course leading to a degree and a college diploma. Such a course gives more scope for practical work but is not primarily a course for performers.

Only three Universities, London, Durham and Dublin award external degrees. Among the several colleges of music which provide full-time courses and examinations for diplomas are:

The Royal Academy of Music, York Gate, Marylebone Road, London, N.W.1. Telephone: 01–935 5461

The Royal College of Music, Prince Consort Road, S. Kensington, London, S.W.7. Telephone: 01–589 3643

The Royal Manchester College of Music, Devas Street, Oxford Road, Manchester 15. Telephone: 061–273 6539

The Royal Scottish Academy of Music, St. George's Place, Glasgow, C.2. Telephone: 041–332 4101

The Royal College of Organists (examinations only), Kensington Gore, London, S.W.7. Telephone: 01–589 1765

The Guildhall School of Music and Drama, Victoria Embankment, London, E.C.4. Telephone: 01–353 7774

Trinity College of Music, London, Mandeville Place, Manchester Square, London, W.1. Telephone: 01–935 5773

The London College of Music, Great Marlborough Street, London W.1. Telephone: 01–437 6120

The Birmingham School of Music, 27 Dale End, Birmingham, 1. Telephone: 021–236 0338

Northern School of Music, Manchester, 91–95a Oxford Road, Manchester, 1. Telephone: 061–273 1844

Dartington College of Arts, Totnes, Devon. Telephone: Totnes 2272.

Other Centres, maintained by L.E.As and catering for all ages, and run either as separate institutions or attached to technical colleges or colleges of further education are listed in the Standing Conference for Amateur Music report (1966) '*Music centres and the training of specially talented children*'.

Most of the full-time courses by these music centres are advertised periodically in the musical press.

Study Abroad: See the Handbook on the subject published by
UNESCO,
Place de Fontenoy,
Paris-7e.

Exchange Visits: For U.S.A. exchanges, details can be obtained from:

> The British Committee for the Interchange of Teachers between the United Kingdom and the United States,
> Dartmouth House,
> 37 Charles Street,
> London, W.1.
> Telephone: 01–629 8995.

For Commonwealth exchanges, from:

> The League of the British Commonwealth and Empire,
> Ord Marshall House,
> 124 Belgrave Road,
> London, S.W.1.
> Telephone: 01–834 0595.

For European exchanges (good qualifications including languages are necessary), from:

> The Central Bureau for Educational Visits and Exchanges,
> 91 Victoria Street,
> London, S.W.1.
> Telephone: 01–799 3941.

The Department of Education and Science (External Relations Branch),

> Curzon Street,
> London, W.1.
> Telephone: 01–493 7070.

publishes an Administrative Memorandum on this subject, and retains overall responsibility for the schemes and will continue to determine the financial conditions applicable to them.

Short Courses: A list of short courses run by the Department of Education and Science is published annually. Many area training organisations and local education authorities run music courses for teachers and there are also a variety of holiday courses covering most aspects of music. Consolidated lists of some of the most important of such courses are published in 'Making Music' and other musical journals.

Examinations, Competitions and Awards

There are seven University Examining Boards, and also the Associated Examining Board, who examine for the General Certificate of Education. All eight include music as a subject at O, A and S levels. Information about these Boards, and also about the fourteen Regional Examinations Boards who examine for the Certificate of Secondary Education may be obtained from:

The Schools Council,
160 Gt. Portland Street,
London, W.1.
Telephone: 01–580 0352

Practical examinations of various grades for individual pupils are arranged at local centres by:

The Associated Board of Royal Schools of Music,
14 Bedford Square,
London, W.C.1.
Telephone: 01–636 4478

Trinity College of Music,
London, Mandeville Place,
Manchester Square,
London, W.1.
Telephone: 01–935 5773

The Guildhall School of Music and Drama,
Victoria Embankment,
London, E.C.4.
Telephone: 01–353 7774

A leaflet listing competitions and awards open to music students is published by the Arts Council.

Broadcasting

British Broadcasting Corporation

Radio and Television Broadcasts to Schools and Colleges are provided by the BBC at the request of the School Broadcasting Council for the United Kingdom. The published Annual Programme contains full information including names and addresses of the Council's Area Education Officers, and can be obtained from:

The Secretary,
School Broadcasting Council for the United Kingdom,
The Langham,
Portland Place,
London, W.1.
Telephone: 01–580 4468

Pupils' pamphlets, teachers' notes and other publications may be obtained from:

The British Broadcasting Corporation,
35 Marylebone High Street,
London, W.1.
Telephone: 01–580 5577

Independent Television

All programmes offered are approved by the Educational Advisory Council of the Independent Television Authority and the Educational Advisory Bodies of the Independent Television Companies.

The published Annual Programme contains addresses of the Company Regions, each of which has a Schools Liaison Officer, and may be obtained from:

The Schools Information Office,
Rediffusion Television Ltd.,
Television House,
Kingsway,
London, W.C.2.
Telephone: 01–405 7888

Copyright

The use of copyright material for education is specifically dealt with in Section 41 of part VI of the Copyright Act, 1956. Copyright in a musical work is not 'taken to be infringed by reason only that the work is reproduced, or an adaptation of the work is made or reproduced.

(a) in the course of instruction, whether at a school or elsewhere, where the reproduction or adaptation is made by a teacher or pupil otherwise than by the use of a duplicating process (*i.e. any process involving the use of an appliance for producing multiple copies is prohibited*), or

(b) as part of the questions to be answered in an examination, or in answer to such a question'.

But this does not apply to gramophone records. Section 12 of the Act specifically states that gramophone records may not lawfully be copied even for private purposes unless the maker's permission has been obtained.

However, the British Record Producers' Association have made valuable concessions for examination purposes. Subject to the strict observance of certain conditions, individual schools, Examining Boards, and the Department of Education and Science may re-record on tapes and discs excerpts not exceeding 60 seconds from commercial records. The agreed conditions are as follows:—

(i) Individual schools

(a) The re-recording must be made on tape;

(b) The tape must be erased after the examination has taken place;

(c) The records from which the tape is made must be the property of the school and purchased through the usual channels.

(ii) Examining Boards and the Department of Education and Science

(a) Up to twenty-five copies of re-recordings may be made on tape; more than twenty-five copies of re-recordings must be made on disc.

(b) Prior permission for re-recording on tape or disc must be obtained from each record manufacturer concerned.

(c) When applying to manufacturers for authority to make discs, the name of the proposed pressing factory must be mentioned.

(d) The labels will have to bear a suitable copyright warning notice and a statement that authority has been obtained to make all the re-recordings.

(e) The discs and tapes will be the property of the Examining Bodies and will remain under their strict control.

(f) The discs will eventually be destroyed, and the tapes must be returned by the schools for erasing after the examination.

(g) The Examining Boards and the Department will be permitted to retain a few copies for reference.

These represent a major concession by the industry and it is only fair to emphasise here that they should be strictly observed.

Enquiries about current agreements should be addressed to:

The Chairman,
British Record Producers Association,
c/o The Copyright Department,
E.M.I. Records,
Blythe Road,
Hayes, Middlesex.

Tapes of school broadcasts may be retained for use until the end of the school year in which they are made. Schools have the right to keep their tape recordings of Radiovision Broadcasts somewhat longer. Details of the current copyright concessions are given in the BBC's annual programme.

Performances of copyright material either 'live' or 'recorded' may not be given in public without permission. School performances are governed by the following extract from the Act:

'Where a literary, dramatic or musical work

> (a) is performed in class, or otherwise in the presence of an audience, and

> (b) is so performed in the course of the activities of a school, by a person who is a teacher in, or a pupil in attendance at, the school,

the performance shall not be taken to be a performance in public if the audience is limited to persons who are teachers in, or pupils in attendance at, the school, or are otherwise directly connected with the activities of the school. A person shall not be taken to be directly connected with the activities of a school by reason only that he is a parent or guardian of a pupil in attendance at the school'.

Further information can be obtained from:

The Performing Rights Society Ltd.,
29–33 Berners Street,
London, W.1.
Telephone: 01–580 5544

who publish a helpful booklet called '*Music and the People*'.

Repertory

Any list of music for use in schools or elsewhere begins to get out-of-date from the day it is written. Only the enterprising teacher who is prepared to search the publishers' lists and send for inspection copies can hope to keep pace with the times. Reviews of new music in the periodicals already listed are a useful guide, however, and it is well worth while for individuals or local schools music associations or festival committees to file them for reference. Teachers should beware of trite music which claims to be specially suited to children. Much fine music written outside the educational field by noted composers is more appropriate.

There are over eighty music-publishing firms in this country, and all of them at some time have in their lists music which teachers may want to use. National Courses usually exhibit wide selections from these and from foreign publishing houses. The addresses of a few well-known publishers are given below:

Ascherberg, Hopwood & Crew Ltd.,
16 Mortimer Street,
London, W.1.
Telephone: 01–636 3562

Edwin Ashdown Ltd.,
19 Hanover Square,
London, W.1.
Telephone: 01–629 1184

Banks & Son (Music) Ltd.,
Stonegate,
York.
Telephone: York 24073

Barenreiter Ltd.,
32/34 Gt. Tichfield Street,
London, W.1.
Telephone: 01–580 9008

Boosey & Hawkes, Music Publishers Ltd.,
295 Regent Street,
London, W.1.
Telephone: 01–580 2060

Bosworth & Co. Ltd.,
14/18 Heddon Street,
Regent Street, London, W.1.
Telephone: 01–734 0475

British & Continental Music Agencies Ltd.,
64 Dean Street,
London, W.1.
Telephone: 01–437 9336

Chappell & Co. Ltd.,
50 New Bond Street,
London, W.1.
Telephone: 01–629 7600

J. & W. Chester Ltd.,
7 Eagle Ct.
London E.C.1.
Telephone: 01–253 6947

J. Curwen & Sons Ltd.,
29 Maiden Lane,
London, W.C.2.
Telephone: 01–240 1666

Galliard Ltd., (Augener),
  148 Charing Cross Road,
  London, W.C.2.
  Telephone: 01–836 9364

Hinrichsen Edition Ltd.,
  Bach House, 10 Baches Street,
  London, N.1.
  Telephone: 01–253 1628

Mills Music Ltd.,
  20 Denmark Street,
  London, W.C.2.
  Telephone: 01–240 1745

Musica Rara,
  2 Gt. Marlborough Street,
  London, W.1.
  Telephone: 01–437 1576

Novello & Co. Ltd.,
  Borough Green,
  Sevenoaks,
  Kent,
  Telephone: Borough Green 3261

Paterson's Ltd.,
  36 Wigmore Street,
  London, W.1.
  Telephone: 01–935 3551

Paxton & Co. Ltd.,
  36–38 Dean Street,
  London, W.1.
  Telephone: 01–437 4801

Keith Prowse Ltd.,
  21 Denmark Street,
  London, W.C.2.
  Telephone: 01–836 3856

Oxford University Press,
  44 Conduit Street, London, W.1.
  Telephone: 01–734 5364

Schott & Co. Ltd.,
  48 Gt. Marlborough Street,
  London, W.1.
  Telephone: 01–437 1246

Stainer & Bell Ltd.,
29 Newman Street, London W.1.
Telephone: 01–636 2558

United Music Publishers,
1 Montague Street, London, W.C.1.
Telephone: 01–636 5171

Universal Edition (London) Ltd.,
2–3 Fareham Street,
Dean Street, London, W.1.
Telephone: 01–437 5203

Libraries

Although many excellent books have been written in recent years about various aspects of music in schools, a bibliography is not included in this chapter as it would so soon become incomplete. Teachers are advised to keep up to date by regularly reading the reviews in at least one appropriate periodical and obtaining books which interest them through their local library. Librarians are always willing to obtain books which are not on their shelves, calling if necessary on the National Central Library, and all will furnish bibliographies. Scores and parts can be borrowed from many local libraries and also, on subscription, from a few larger music libraries such as the Henry Watson Library in Manchester.

Catalogues of commercial hire libraries may be obtained from:

Boosey & Hawkes,
Music Publishers,
295 Regent Street, London, W.1.

J. & W. Chester Ltd.,
7 Eagle Court, London, E.C.1.

Goodwin & Tabb Ltd.,
36–38 Dean Street, London, W.1. Telephone: Gerrard 1574.

Places of Musical Interest

(a) Visits to factories and workshops manufacturing musical instruments can usually be made after prior arrangements with the proprietors. Examples of such firms are:—

Boosey & Hawkes, Ltd.,
Deansbrook Road,
Edgware, Middlesex.
(Modern orchestral instruments)

Arnold Dolmetsch Ltd.,
Beechside, Grayswood Road,
Haslemere, Surrey.
(Keyboard and stringed instruments and recorders)

Hele & Co. Ltd.,
  4a Alma Villas,
  Plymouth.
    (Organs)

Robert Morley & Co. Ltd.,
  Morley Galleries,
  4 Belmont Hill,
  Lewisham, London, S.E. 13.
    and workshops at:
  Ringers Road,
  Bromley, Kent.
    (Pianos, harpsichords and clavichords)

Premier Drum Co. Ltd.,
  87 Regent Street,
  London, W.1.
    and factory at:
  Canal Street,
  South Wigston, Leicester.

Rushworth & Dreaper Ltd.,
  42–46 Whitechapel,
  Liverpool, 1.
    (Organs)

J. W. Walker & Sons, Ltd.,
  Braintree Road (off Victoria Road),
  Ruislip, Middlesex.
    (Organs)

(b) Museums and private collections. (Since opening times and conditions of admission vary considerably, it is advisable to check arrangements prior to visiting).

Ashmolean Museum, Beaumont Street, Oxford.
  (English and Italian stringed instruments)

Brighton Art Gallery and Museum, Church Street, Brighton, 1.
  (The Albert Spencer Collection)

The British Museum, Bloomsbury, London, W.C.1.
  (Oriental and primitive instruments, and collections of musical manuscripts).

The British Piano Museum, 36B High Street, Brentford, Middlesex.

Carisbrooke Castle Museum, Newport, Isle-of-Wight.
  (Contains the oldest organ in the country)

The Royal College of Music (Donaldson Museum), Prince Consort Road, South Kensington, London, S.W.7.

Fenton House (The National Trust), Hampstead Grove, London, N.W.3.
(Early keyboard instruments)

The Fitzwilliam Museum, Trumpington Street, Cambridge.
(Collections of music and mediaeval manuscripts)

Geffrye Museum, Kingsland Road, Shoreditch, London, E.2.

Heaton Hall, Heaton Park, Manchester.
(The music room)

The Horniman Museum, London Road, S.E.23.
(Over 4,000 exhibits from all parts of the world)

The Mickleburgh Collection of Musical Instruments, 1–7 Stokes Croft, Bristol.

The Pitt Rivers Museum, Parks Road, Oxford.
(5,000 instruments including autophones)

The Rushworth and Dreaper Permanent Collection of Antique Musical Instruments, 42–46 Whitechapel, Liverpool, 1.

Snowshill Manor (The National Trust), Broadway, Gloucestershire.

Tolson Memorial Museum, Ravensknowle Park, Huddersfield.
(A wide variety from an ophicleide to a street organ)

Victoria and Albert Museum, Cromwell Road, London, S.W.7.
(Craftsmanship in antique instruments)

Welsh Folk Museum, St. Fagan's Castle, Glamorgan.

The William Barrow Collection of Antique Musical Instruments and Books, 'Nant-y-Clyn', Church Walks, Llandudno.

The Cornwall Music Centre, St. Keyne, near Liskeard, Cornwall.
(Private collection of pipe organs and mechanical instruments)

General information can be obtained from the Museums Association, 87 Charlotte Street, London, W.1.
Telephone: 01–636 4600.

Printed for Her Majesty's Stationery Office by Hobbs the Printers Ltd. Southampton
(1323) D.138587 K60 12/68 G3313

SBN 11 270088 8

Noye shuts the window of the Ark.

73 (Thunder & lightning)

Computational Methods for the Solution of Engineering Problems

3rd revised edition

C. A. Brebbia and
A. J. Ferrante